PREVENTION, DE-ESCALATION, AND RESILIENCE (PDR)

Strategies for Navigating Adversity

Sheila Mallett-Smith and Jiles Smith II

Published by Isham Media Group LLC

The Smith & Smith Collaborative

Table of Contents

Preface

This book grew out of a simple observation we kept hearing from good people doing hard work: the job keeps getting heavier, but the tools for handling the emotional weight have not kept up.

In schools, hospitals, clinics, city departments, social service agencies, and other public-facing settings, conflict is not an occasional disruption. It is often a daily visitor. It shows up as frustration, disrespect, withdrawal, tears, threats, complaints, and sometimes violence. It also shows up in quieter ways, such as moral injury, burnout, and a steady erosion of trust between the people we serve and those trying to help.

We wrote this to be practical. Not in the sense of quick tips that ignore reality, but in the sense of guidance you can actually use when things are tense, and you have limited time and support. Our core belief is that most escalation is predictable. That does not mean every incident can be prevented, but it does mean you can learn to spot patterns earlier, respond more skillfully, and build systems that reduce harm over time.

We also wrote this to be humane. Prevention, de-escalation, and resilience are not only professional competencies. There are ways of protecting dignity, including your own. If a workplace culture expects people to absorb conflict without recovery, it will eventually break people down, no matter how committed they are.

Our hope is that you will use this framework in three directions at once. First, with the people you serve, by shaping conditions that reduce unnecessary stress. Second, with your teams, by building shared language and shared responses so no one is left to improvise alone. Third, with your organizations, by aligning policy, training, and leadership practices with how human nervous systems actually function.

If you take one idea with you before you even turn the page, let it be this: conflict is information. It is often a signal that safety, clarity, or connection is missing. When we treat it that way, we stop chasing symptoms and start improving conditions.

Thank you for the work you do, and for the people you serve.

Introduction

I've spoken with educators who quietly cry in their cars before walking into a classroom. Nurses who finish a twelve-hour shift only to return home and care for others. Social workers who carry the weight of a dozen crises in their inbox. Front desk staff who smile politely while absorbing the frustrations of systems too stretched to serve everyone well.

These professionals work in public-facing roles where the stakes are high, emotions run deep, and the margin for error is thin.

They rarely complain. Yet the signs are there—in their body language, in the way they speak about "just getting through the day," and in the long pause before they answer when asked, How are you holding up?

These are not isolated moments of burnout. They are symptoms of systems under sustained pressure. They are unfolding across schools, hospitals, mental health agencies, family services, probation departments, call centers, and any setting where people show up daily to meet the needs of others while managing their own stress and uncertainty.

What we are witnessing is not a lack of commitment. It is a lack of sustainable support.

The people doing the most emotionally demanding work often have the fewest tools to recover, the fewest spaces to reflect, and the greatest exposure to conflict, trauma, and chronic strain. When institutions fail to account for this reality, escalation becomes routine, burnout becomes normalized, and safety becomes fragile for everyone involved.

That is where this book begins.

A Shared Human Challenge

Adversity is not limited to childhood, crisis, or catastrophe. It emerges across the lifespan and across professional environments. While its causes vary, research shows that the human nervous system responds to psychological threat in remarkably consistent ways, whether that threat comes from early trauma, workplace instability, or repeated exposure to others' distress.

Stress reshapes how people think, feel, and relate. It narrows attention, heightens reactivity, and makes communication more difficult precisely when clarity and connection are most needed. Over time, unresolved stress alters not only individual behavior, but the culture of entire organizations.

This is why challenges that appear interpersonal are often systemic. A tense exchange with a parent, a patient who lashes out, a colleague who withdraws, or a student who escalates is rarely just about the moment itself. These interactions carry the weight of accumulated strain, unmet needs, and environments that have not been designed for regulation and safety.

Understanding this reality shifts the question from What's wrong with this person? to What conditions shaped this response?

A Framework for Safety and Sustainability

This book offers a structured, research-informed framework for addressing adversity in high-stress, people-centered environments. That framework rests on three interdependent pillars:

Prevention, De-escalation, and Resilience.

These are not isolated strategies. They are complementary processes that work together to support both individuals and systems over time.

Prevention focuses on shaping conditions that reduce the likelihood of escalation before it begins. This includes attention to environment, communication, routines, leadership practices, and policies that influence how safe people feel in their daily interactions. Prevention is proactive and intentional. It asks how we can design spaces, relationships, and systems that support regulation rather than threat.

De-escalation addresses what happens when tension rises despite our best efforts. It is the practice of restoring safety in the moment through presence, communication, and co-regulation. De-escalation requires understanding how stress affects the brain and body, and how professionals can remain grounded while helping others return to balance.

Resilience focuses on what happens after adversity. It concerns recovery, reflection, and growth. Resilience is not about endurance alone. It is about creating conditions that allow individuals and organizations to adapt, learn, and remain healthy over time. Without resilience, prevention and de-escalation cannot be sustained.

Together, these three pillars form a continuum of care for both people and systems.

A Social Ecological Lens

At the core of this approach is the Social Ecological Model, which recognizes that stress and behavior are shaped by multiple interacting layers:

- Individual (personal history, emotional regulation, lived experience)
- Interpersonal (relationships with colleagues, clients, supervisors, and families)
- Environmental (physical space, sensory cues, accessibility, predictability)
- Organizational (policies, leadership culture, training structures)
- Systemic (equity, funding, social expectations, and institutional norms)

This model allows us to see conflict and distress not as isolated failures, but as signals emerging from interconnected systems. It also reveals where intervention can occur. Prevention may begin with environmental and organizational design. De-escalation unfolds in interpersonal moments. Resilience depends on individual and collective recovery processes.

No single layer is sufficient on its own. Sustainable change requires alignment across all of them.

Beyond Self-Care

What is needed is more than another reminder to practice self-care. While individual strategies matter, they are insufficient without supportive structures. People cannot regulate in environments that continually signal threat. They cannot recover in systems that reward exhaustion. And they cannot remain resilient when reflection and repair are absent from organizational life.

This book argues for a shift from reactive models of crisis management toward integrated approaches that address biological, psychological, and social dimensions of adversity. It is grounded in neuroscience, trauma-informed practice, and public health perspectives, but it is written for those who live this work every day.

The framework presented here is not industry-specific. It is human-specific.

It is for educators navigating classrooms shaped by trauma and inequity.

It is for healthcare workers caring for patients while carrying their own emotional burden.

It is for public servants, social workers, and frontline staff who serve communities under strain.

It is for anyone whose job requires emotional presence in difficult circumstances.

What This Book Offers

Throughout this book, you will encounter research, case examples, and practical strategies designed to help you:

- recognize environmental and relational triggers of escalation
- use de-escalation tools that restore safety and dignity
- build individual and organizational resilience over time
- assess how systems distribute stress and support regulation

- develop practices that align policy with human neuro-biology

This is not a manual for perfection. It is a framework for awareness, intention, and growth.

A Time of Strain and Possibility

We are living in a period of collective strain. Social systems are stretched. Public-facing professions carry increasing emotional labor. Conflict has become more visible, and patience more fragile.

But this is also a time of collective possibility.

When adversity is understood rather than denied, when stress is addressed rather than moralized, and when systems are designed with the nervous system in mind, new patterns can emerge. Safety can be cultivated. Communication can improve. Recovery can be normalized.

By embracing prevention, practicing de-escalation, and committing to resilience, we can create workplaces that are not only functional, but humane.

Not only efficient, but sustainable.

Not only responsive, but wise.

This book is an invitation to rethink how we understand stress, how we respond to conflict, and how we care for those who care for others.

The chapters that follow begin by examining the foundations of conflict itself—how stress, trauma, and systems shape behavior—before turning to prevention, de-escalation, and resilience as practical, evidence-based responses.

SECTION 1

PREVENTION

Chapter 1

The Foundations of Conflict

Neurobiology, Stress, and Systems in High-Stress Environments

More Than Just a Disagreement

Conflict is often framed as a simple disagreement, but in high-stress environments, where emotions, trauma, and responsibility collide, it is rarely just that. In public-facing professions such as education, healthcare, and social services, conflict frequently carries deep emotional undertones and feels personally charged. A misinterpreted comment, a disagreement over policy, or a tense exchange with a frustrated parent or patient can quickly spiral in settings where everyone is already operating near their emotional limits. These experiences are not uncommon, and they are not always the result of poor communication. More often, they are the product of accumulated stress, trauma histories, and strained systems.

Bruce Perry and colleagues[1] describe how individuals with histories of trauma may interpret everyday interactions as threatening, reacting from survival brain states rather than calm, reflective thinking. This dynamic not only affects children or clients. It appears in professionals as well. When stress becomes chronic and support is limited, even highly experienced workers can find themselves caught in reactive cycles that undermine judgment, empathy, and connection.

Importantly, baseline stress is not distributed evenly. Research on Adverse Childhood Experiences (ACEs) demonstrates that early exposure to abuse, neglect, or household instability sensitizes stress-response systems over time[2,3]. More recent work expands this understanding by emphasizing that early adversity is often paired with ongoing environmental stressors—what Ellis and colleagues describe as Adverse Community Environments— including community violence, housing instability, discrimination, and systemic inequities[4]. Together, these paired adversities increase vulnerability to heightened threat perception in everyday interactions.

These stress-loaded nervous systems, whether shaped by early life experience, current environment, or both, help explain why seemingly minor workplace interactions can escalate rapidly in high-stress professional settings. This does not indicate weakness or poor intent. Rather, it reflects how human neurobiology adapts to sustained adversity.

Defining Conflict in High-Stress Environments

In these contexts, conflict is more than a disagreement. It is a signal of deeper disconnection. It emerges when perceived needs, goals, or values clash, often shaped by internalized stress or unresolved trauma[5]. In trauma-exposed environments, the roots of conflict are layered, tied to past wounds, present pressures, and limited emotional bandwidth.

The ACEs framework has long established the relationship between early exposure to abuse, neglect, and household dysfunction and long-term outcomes related to health, behavior, and emotional regulation[2,3]. However, ACEs alone do not fully explain the patterns of stress, vigilance, and conflict observed in many contemporary settings. Ellis[6] expands this understanding through the concept of Adverse Community Environments, highlighting how exposure to community violence, systemic racism, housing instability, under-resourced schools, environmental hazards, and chronic economic stress compounds the impact of ACEs across the lifespan.

Together, ACEs and Adverse Community Environments operate as a paired exposure—one rooted in early relational experience and the other in sustained environmental stress. This pairing helps explain why conflict is often more intense, persistent, and difficult to resolve in communities and workplaces shaped by structural inequity and chronic instability. In such contexts, conflict may represent not a failure of skill, but an adaptive response to long-standing conditions of threat.

Conflict does not always appear as yelling or overt hostility. It may present as silence, withdrawal, or avoidance, subtle symptoms of emotional exhaustion or mistrust. These "quiet" conflicts are no less damaging. They erode trust, compromise collaboration, and leave emotional residues that weaken team cohesion[3].

Miscommunication, often exacerbated by digital platforms, unclear tone, or ambiguous expectations, plays a substantial role in fueling conflict. Treviño et al.[7] emphasize the importance of clarity and empathy in communication to reduce misunderstandings, especially in fast-paced or emotionally charged environments. When communication lacks relational safety, even neutral messages can be perceived as threatening.

Understanding this complexity matters. Unaddressed conflict can fester and deepen divisions, particularly in professions where the stakes, whether child safety, patient care, public safety, or family stability, are high.

The Role of Emotional Triggers and Stress Responses

The neurobiology of stress helps explain why conflict can escalate so rapidly in high-pressure roles. The amygdala, often referred to as the brain's alarm system, is designed to detect threat and activate survival responses before the rational brain has time to evaluate the situation[8]. In environments characterized by chronic stress, individuals are more vulnerable to "amygdala hijacks," episodes of emotional reactivity that override logic and reflection.

Perry et al.[9] demonstrated that repeated exposure to trauma and toxic stress alters the developing brain, particularly in regions responsible for regulation, impulse control, and relational safety. While this research is often applied to children, it is equally relevant to adults experiencing cumulative stress or compassion fatigue. For these individuals, seemingly minor incidents can provoke outsized emotional responses.

Anxiety related to organizational instability or client volatility is frequently a hidden but potent trigger. According to the American Psychological Association[10], anxiety manifests physically (muscle tension, fatigue), emotionally (irritability, fear), and cognitively (difficulty concentrating), complicating interpersonal interactions in the workplace.

Salo and colleagues[10] further note that sustained exposure to others' trauma can result in vicarious traumatization, particularly when support systems are weak. The emotional labor required in public-facing professions—constantly caring for others while navigating bureaucratic constraints—leaves professionals depleted and vulnerable to reactivity.

Neurobiological Embedding of Conflict Across Contexts

Contemporary neuroscience demonstrates that chronic adversity produces measurable changes in brain structure and function across populations. Prolonged stress is associated with reductions in prefrontal cortex capacity, enlargement of the amygdala, and disruption of hippocampal functioning[11,12,13]. These changes impair executive functioning, heighten threat sensitivity, and weaken emotional regulation.

Remarkably, these neural patterns appear consistently across diverse groups. Individuals with high ACE scores, healthcare providers experiencing burnout, and workers exposed to organizational instability all show similar stress-related neurological profiles. This biological commonality explains why core prevention and regulation strategies can be effective across schools, hospitals, and workplaces.

Neuroplasticity offers a parallel message of hope. Environments marked by safety, predictability, and relational attunement strengthen regulatory neural pathways and buffer physiological stress activation across the lifespan[14]. Consistent, supportive relationships contribute to this recalibration by reinforcing integration between emotional and executive brain systems. Conflict, viewed through this lens, reflects dysregulated stress circuitry rather than defective character.

Cultural, Organizational, and Systemic Influences

Context matters. Organizational culture, policy, and leadership approaches shape how conflict arises and whether it is resolved constructively. In some systems, open communication is discouraged or unsafe. In others, collaboration is promoted rhetorically but not structurally supported.

Cultural norms also influence how conflict is expressed and interpreted. What one individual views as assertiveness may be perceived by another as aggression, depending on cultural background and communication style[16]. Without training in cultural humility, these mismatches can escalate quickly.

The Social Ecological Model[17,18] explains how layers of influence, individual, interpersonal, environmental, organizational, and systemic, interact to shape behavior. Conflict is rarely an individual problem. It is often an emergent property of systems that unintentionally reinforce competition, inequity, or survival-based responses.

Organizations serving communities affected by concentrated disadvantage frequently operate under heightened demand, limited resources, and increased trauma exposure. When institutional policies fail to account for this reality, conflict becomes predictable rather than exceptional.

Understanding conflict through the paired lens of ACEs and Adverse Community Environments shifts attention away from individual blame and toward systemic responsibility. Prevention must therefore be trauma-informed, equity-centered, and responsive to lived realities.

Why Understanding Conflict Is Foundational

Conflict is not inherently negative. It can serve as a catalyst for growth when approached with awareness and skill. To leverage conflict constructively, professionals must first understand its neurobiological roots, emotional dimensions, and systemic context.

When conflict is recognized as communication of unmet needs, emotional, relational, or structural, responses can shift from defensiveness to curiosity. Instead of reacting or withdrawing, professionals can engage with empathy and accountability.

This chapter establishes the foundation for the framework that follows. By examining conflict through a trauma-informed and systems-based lens, it becomes possible to see it not simply as a problem to fix, but as an opportunity to understand, connect, and redesign environments for safety and regulation.

From Conflict to Prevention: A Systems-Based Scientific Imperative

Contemporary neuroscience and public health research converge on a central conclusion: conflict is not merely an interpersonal problem, but a predictable expression of neurobiological stress interacting with relational and environmental systems. Chronic adversity produces measurable changes in brain structure and function, including reductions in prefrontal cortex capacity, enlargement of the amygdala, and disruption of hippocampal integration processes[11,12,13]. These patterns appear consistently across populations exposed to sustained stress, whether through childhood trauma, healthcare burnout, or organizational instability.

Importantly, these stress-related adaptations are not fixed. Neuroplastic processes allow recalibration when systems are intentionally structured around safety, relational consistency, and predictability[14]. This scientific insight carries organizational implications: prevention is not achieved through correction after harm, but through the deliberate design of environments that reduce chronic threat activation. When stress physiology is addressed at the systems level, conflict becomes less frequent, less intense, and more repairable.

These insights demand a shift from reactive models of discipline and crisis management toward preventive, trauma-informed design. Public health paradigms consistently show that multilevel interventions targeting biological, psychological, and social systems yield greater impact than strategies focused solely on individual behavior[19]. Prevention thus becomes a collective responsibility, requiring attention to how environments distribute stress, how policies communicate meaning, and how organizational cultures shape nervous system regulation.

The next chapter examines prevention not as avoidance of conflict, but as the intentional construction of conditions that support emotional regulation, relational safety, and predictable structure. By aligning neuroscience with organizational practice, prevention becomes the first and most powerful form of de-escalation.

Chapter 2

Cultivating a Prevention Mindset

Behavior, Meaning, and Communication in High-Stress Systems

Conflict rarely appears without warning. As established in Chapter 1, escalation reflects predictable interactions between neurobiology, lived experience, and the conditions of the system itself. When a threat is perceived, stress physiology shifts perception and narrows cognitive flexibility, and these effects are amplified in environments marked by uncertainty, inconsistency, and relational rupture[13,12,8]. A prevention mindset begins upstream, by recognizing early signals of dysregulation and shaping conditions that reduce threat, restore predictability, and preserve dignity before conflict becomes visible.

In high-stress professional environments such as education, healthcare, and public service, individuals operate under sustained cognitive and emotional load. When a threat is perceived, the amygdala activates and access to prefrontal reasoning narrows, reducing empathy, impulse control, and verbal communication[8,11]. Behavior that appears oppositional or disengaged may therefore reflect an adaptive survival response rather than intentional misconduct. A prevention mindset begins with recognizing that escalation is rarely sudden. It is the cumulative result of unaddressed stress, misinterpretation, and unmet relational needs.

Understanding behavior as communication requires a fundamental shift in interpretive stance. Rather than asking how to suppress problematic conduct, a prevention framework asks what the behavior reveals about the individual's experience of safety, power, or belonging. This perspective does not eliminate accountability but reframes professional responses toward early recognition and regulation. When behavior is treated as information rather than defiance, professionals gain access to intervention points that precede crisis.

Behavior as Communication in High-Stress Systems

Human behavior reflects the interaction between internal emotional states and external conditions. Trauma and chronic adversity sensitize the stress-response system, increasing vigilance and narrowing tolerance for ambiguity[2,3,6]. Under such conditions, minor interpersonal exchanges may be experienced as threatening. A raised voice may signal panic rather than aggression. Withdrawal may signal shame rather than apathy. Anger may reflect fear of being dismissed or unheard.

Neurobiological research confirms that chronic adversity produces stress-related changes that compromise executive functioning, heighten threat sensitivity, and disrupt memory integration[12,11]. Functionally, this means the same environment can feel manageable to one person and unsafe to another depending on stress load and prior exposure. These neural patterns appear across childhood adversity, healthcare burnout, and organizational trauma, suggesting that prevention strategies must address universal stress mechanisms rather than context-specific behaviors alone.

Interpretation shapes outcome. When behavior is interpreted as intentional misconduct, responses tend to escalate. When behavior is interpreted as stress communication, responses are more likely to stabilize. Attribution errors such as assuming malicious intent activate defensiveness and narrow the range of professional responses. Curiosity, by contrast, broadens interpretation and opens space for proportional, dignity-preserving intervention.

This interpretive shift does not deny responsibility. It reframes responsibility as shared rather than adversarial. Boundaries remain necessary, but they are communicated as stabilizing structures rather than punitive judgments. In this way, prevention becomes relational rather than reactive.

A Social Ecological Framework for Prevention

Prevention is not an individual trait. It is a system property. A social ecological framework recognizes that escalation is shaped not only by personal history but by relationships, organizational structures, and community conditions[17,18]. Individuals do not escalate in isolation. They escalate within systems that may buffer or amplify stress.

Bronfenbrenner's model emphasizes nested levels of influence, including interpersonal relationships, institutional policies, and cultural norms. Mallett-Smith et al.[18] extend this framework by situating escalation within intersecting systems of personal experience, workplace climate, and community stress. From this perspective, behavior reflects both internal state and environmental design.

This approach aligns with public health paradigms, demonstrating that multilevel interventions targeting biological, psychological, and social systems are more effective than single-focus strategies[19]. Seen this way, prevention becomes a collective responsibility. It requires attention to how environments distribute stress and how institutions communicate meaning.

Paired Adversity: ACEs and Adverse Community Environments

The Adverse Childhood Experiences (ACE) study established a graded relationship between early trauma and lifelong health and behavioral outcomes[2,20]. Ellis[6] expanded this framework by introducing the concept of Adverse Community Environments, including exposure to violence, discrimination, housing instability, and chronic poverty. These two forms of adversity function as paired exposures, one rooted in early relational experience and the other in sustained environmental stress.

Together, ACEs and Adverse Community Environments heighten sensitivity to perceived threat. Chronic exposure to instability conditions the nervous system to anticipate danger. Hypervigilance becomes adaptive. Emotional reactivity becomes protective. What appears as defiance or withdrawal in professional settings may represent survival strategies learned in unsafe environments.

This paired framework explains why conflict is often more intense and persistent in communities shaped by structural inequity. In such contexts, escalation reflects not a failure of skill but an adaptive response to longstanding conditions of threat. For prevention to hold, institutional humility and systemic responsibility must replace individual blame.

Meaning-Making and Interpretation

Stress is not defined solely by events. It is defined by interpretation. Two people may experience the same interaction and respond very differently based on history, culture, and identity. Meaning-making lies at the center of escalation.

Individuals assign meaning to tone, posture, and language through the lens of prior experience. A directive may be interpreted as guidance by one person and as humiliation by another. Trauma alters this interpretive lens, biasing perception toward danger[21]. Cultural background further shapes meaning. What one culture views as assertive, another may perceive as disrespectful[22].

Neurodivergence and sensory sensitivity add additional layers of complexity. Overstimulation may be mistaken for defiance. Communication differences may be misread as avoidance. Without awareness of these dynamics, misinterpretation becomes a primary pathway to escalation.

Prevention requires slowing interpretation. It involves asking not only what happened, but what the interaction meant to the person experiencing it. This shift from certainty to curiosity is among the most powerful preventive interventions available.

Communication as the Primary Tool of Prevention

Prevention is fundamentally communicative. Long before conflict escalates into behavioral disruption or crisis, individuals are sending signals about stress, threat perception, unmet needs, and emotional load. These signals may appear as resistance, withdrawal, irritability, or disengagement, yet they function as early warning indicators of dysregulation rather than intentional opposition. A prevention-oriented culture trains professionals to interpret behavior as communication rather than provocation.

Neuroscience confirms that communication is not merely verbal but relational and physiological. Tone of voice, facial expression, body posture, and pacing are processed by the nervous system more rapidly than spoken language[8]. Individuals operating from threat states are highly sensitive to perceived judgment, authority, and unpredictability. When communication conveys safety, predictability, and respect, it can stabilize the nervous system before conflict emerges. When communication conveys criticism, urgency, or ambiguity, it can activate threat responses even when no danger exists.

Effective prevention communication is not a technique but a stance. It is grounded in curiosity rather than correction and assumes that behavior has logic rooted in experience. This approach aligns with trauma-informed frameworks that emphasize voice, choice, and collaboration[7]. In classrooms, healthcare settings, and public-facing workplaces, this stance transforms everyday interactions into opportunities for regulation rather than escalation.

In her public presentation on trauma-informed schools, Crnobori[16] emphasizes that prevention depends on relational consistency. When adults respond to stress with predictable language and emotional steadiness, individuals learn what to expect from the environment. Predictability reduces cognitive load and builds trust, particularly for those with histories of adversity. Over time, this relational predictability functions as a buffer against reactive cycles.

Communication as prevention also requires abandoning deficit-based language. Phrases such as "noncompliant," "defiant," or "attention-seeking" obscure the adaptive purpose of behavior. Trauma-informed language reframes these observations into functional descriptions: seeking connection, avoiding threat, or attempting control in an overwhelming context. This linguistic shift alters not only professional attitudes but also institutional culture.

Savannah Lynn Armistead's[23] work on trauma-informed practices in pre-service teacher training demonstrates that when educators are taught to interpret behavior through a neurodevelopmental lens, disciplinary referrals decrease while student engagement improves. This finding reinforces that prevention begins not with policy enforcement but with perception. How professionals interpret behavior determines how they respond to it.

Communication operates continuously as a regulatory force within organizations, shaping emotional climate through tone, timing, and meaning long before conflict becomes overt.

Language, Listening, and Repair

Communication is not merely the transmission of information. It is the primary mechanism through which safety or threat is conveyed. Everyday language shapes emotional climate. Tone, pacing, and word choice regulate nervous systems long before policy or consequence is invoked.

Active listening functions as a preventive intervention. When individuals feel heard, their stress response diminishes. Research in relational neuroscience demonstrates that attuned listening activates neural pathways associated with safety and social engagement[8,24]. Conversely, interruption and dismissal activate defensive circuitry. Prevention depends on communication practices that validate emotion without endorsing harmful behavior.

Empathy operates as threat reduction. It does not require agreement. It requires recognition. Statements that acknowledge frustration or confusion signal that the individual's internal state has been registered. This recognition alone often reduces physiological arousal and restores access to reflective thought.

Repair is equally essential. Miscommunication is inevitable. What distinguishes prevention-oriented systems is not the absence of rupture but the presence of repair. When misunderstandings are acknowledged and addressed respectfully, trust is restored and future escalation becomes less likely. In prevention-oriented systems, repair is treated as routine maintenance rather than crisis intervention.

Language also constructs institutional meaning. Communication that frames conflict as failure fosters shame. Communication that frames conflict as information fosters learning. Over time, these narratives shape whether individuals experience systems as adversarial or supportive.

Digital Communication and Escalation Risk

Digital platforms amplify misinterpretation by removing relational cues such as tone, facial expression, and immediacy. Email and messaging systems often compress complex emotional content into brief textual exchanges. In high-stress environments, this compression increases the likelihood that neutral messages will be perceived as hostile.

Treviño et al.[7] found that ambiguity in digital communication heightens emotional reactivity, particularly in environments characterized by power differentials. In this framework, prevention-oriented systems establish norms that emphasize clarity, tone awareness, and opportunities for clarification. Emotionally charged issues require voice or face-to-face interaction whenever possible.

Digital communication is not neutral. It is part of the emotional environment. How institutions use it either stabilizes or destabilizes relationships.

Table 1
Interpretation vs. Prevention-Oriented Response

Feature	Escalation-Oriented Interpretation	Prevention-Oriented Interpretation

View of behavior	Violation	Communication
Emotional stance	Judgment	Curiosity
Language	Command-based	Relational
Outcome	Defensiveness	Regulation
System effect	Instability	Predictability

Prevention as a System Property

Prevention cannot be sustained solely through individual skill. While professional competence and emotional awareness matter, they are insufficient when embedded within systems that amplify stress, confusion, or inequity. A prevention mindset requires a shift from viewing escalation as an individual failure to understanding it as a systemic signal. Organizations communicate values not only through formal statements but through daily routines, policies, and leadership behaviors. These structures shape how stress is interpreted and how meaning is constructed long before conflict becomes visible.

Organizational research demonstrates that institutional support systems account for the majority of variance in outcomes related to stress regulation and behavioral stability[25]. This finding reframes prevention as a collective responsibility rather than a personal burden. Policies that emphasize predictability, fairness, and relational accountability function as upstream regulators of emotional climate. In contrast, systems marked by inconsistency or punitive reflexes increase threat perception and reduce the likelihood of calm engagement.

When prevention is treated as a system property, safety is no longer dependent on heroic individual effort. Communication norms become shared. Over time, responses become more predictable. Dignity becomes embedded in procedure rather than contingent on personality. This systemic approach does not eliminate conflict, but it alters how conflict unfolds. Stress becomes something to be addressed rather than punished, and meaning becomes something to be explored rather than imposed.

Training as Cultural Transmission

Training is one of the primary vehicles through which organizations transmit their values. It does more than convey information. It shapes professional identity. When training focuses exclusively on crisis response or rule enforcement, it implicitly teaches that safety begins only after disruption occurs. A prevention-oriented training framework teaches that safety begins with interpretation, presence, and relational awareness.

Effective prevention training integrates knowledge of stress neurobiology, behavior as communication, relational buffering, and social ecological context. It equips professionals to recognize early indicators of distress and to respond in ways that stabilize rather than escalate. Over time, these practices become shared language rather than isolated techniques.

Training also functions as cultural reinforcement. One-time workshops do not create prevention cultures. Culture is built through repetition and modeling. When supervisors and leaders use prevention language in daily interactions, training becomes embodied rather than theoretical. When prevention principles are referenced in supervision, documentation, and policy, they become institutional memory.

Importantly, prevention training must address communication explicitly. Professionals must be supported in developing skills of active listening, empathetic inquiry, and repair. These are not soft skills. They are regulatory tools. Language can either activate or calm the nervous system. Teaching professionals how to speak in ways that preserve dignity is, in practice, a form of biological intervention.

Meaning-Making Through Policy and Practice

Policies are forms of communication. They tell individuals what is valued, what is feared, and what is expected. Prevention requires that policies align with relational and biological realities. When policies emphasize control without context, they inadvertently increase stress and reduce trust. When policies emphasize proportionality and fairness, they function as stabilizing structures.

Meaning-making occurs through consistency. Predictable responses reduce uncertainty, which is one of the primary drivers of threat perception. In contrast, inconsistent enforcement generates anxiety and hypervigilance. Individuals become more concerned with avoiding punishment than with understanding expectations. This requires coherence between values, training, and policy.

Documentation systems also shape meaning. Records that capture only violations communicate judgment. Records that include context and repair communicate understanding. Over time, these practices influence how professionals interpret behavior and how individuals experience authority.

Ethical Foundations of Prevention

Prevention is not only a practical strategy. It is an ethical commitment. Treating behavior as communication acknowledges human complexity. Designing systems that reduce threat reflects respect for vulnerability. Preserving dignity during stress affirms human worth.

Ethical prevention asks fundamental questions: Do institutional practices create safety or fear? Do they reduce harm or reproduce it? Do they invite understanding or enforce silence? These questions ground prevention in values rather than convenience.

Ellis[6] emphasizes that Adverse Community Environments disproportionately affect marginalized populations. Institutions serving such communities carry an ethical responsibility to avoid replicating dynamics of control and punishment that mirror external stressors. That commitment includes cultural humility and attention to structural inequities.

Equity also demands that responses be proportional and contextual. Policies that appear neutral may have unequal impact. Zero-tolerance approaches disproportionately affect individuals already exposed to trauma and instability. Prevention-oriented systems replace rigid uniformity with fairness grounded in human experience.

Leadership and Organizational Meaning

Leadership functions as emotional architecture within organizations. Leaders model how stress is interpreted and how conflict is handled. Their responses teach others what is safe and what is dangerous.

Trauma-informed leadership emphasizes consistency, transparency, and proportionality[26]. Consistency reduces uncertainty. Transparency reduces suspicion. Proportionality ensures that responses match the level of concern rather than amplifying it unnecessarily.

Leaders also determine whether prevention becomes embedded or remains aspirational. When leaders prioritize relational safety alongside performance, they signal that emotional well-being is not secondary to productivity. This alignment is particularly critical in environments shaped by high levels of adversity.

Supervision practices further communicate meaning. Reflective supervision supports professionals in examining their own emotional responses and interpretive habits. It frames challenges as learning opportunities rather than failures. This approach preserves dignity and strengthens regulatory capacity.

Table 2

Communication as Prevention Across System Levels

Level	Escalation-Oriented Practice	Prevention-Oriented Practice
Individual	Command and correction	Listening and validation
Interpersonal	Blame	Curiosity
Organizational	Zero tolerance	Proportional response
Leadership	Reactive	Reflective
Culture	Fear-based	Dignity-based

Integration Across Levels of Influence

A prevention mindset requires alignment across individual, relational, organizational, and community levels. The social ecological framework clarifies that no single intervention is sufficient. Individual regulation must be supported by relational safety, and relational safety must be reinforced by policy coherence. Policy coherence must be informed by community context.

When these levels operate in alignment, prevention becomes self-reinforcing. Individuals experience less threat. Professionals retain regulatory capacity. Institutions maintain stability. When these levels operate in contradiction, escalation becomes likely regardless of individual skill.

Prevention is not a program but a pattern. It is reflected in how people speak, how policies are written, and how leaders respond to stress. Over time, these patterns shape whether escalation is the exception or the norm.

Closing Synthesis

Cultivating a prevention mindset begins with how behavior is understood and how meaning is constructed. When professionals view conflict as communication rather than defiance, they gain access to early intervention. When organizations adopt a social ecological framework, they recognize that behavior is shaped by context as much as by choice.

Communication operates as a central prevention tool. Active listening, empathy, and repair regulate nervous systems and preserve dignity. Policies and leadership practices reinforce these messages through consistency and proportionality. Ethics and equity guide how power is exercised and how stress is distributed.

Prevention is not the avoidance of adversity. It is the intentional design of systems that support human capacity in the face of adversity. By shifting from reaction to interpretation, from punishment to meaning-making, and from control to connection, organizations reduce the likelihood that stress will evolve into crisis.

The next chapter examines the mechanisms that convert stress into escalation in real time, including state-dependent perception, dignity and shame dynamics, and emotional regulation as a trained capacity.

Chapter 3

Trauma-Informed Prevention

Neurobiology, Meaning-Making, and the Escalation Continuum

Trauma-Informed Prevention: Neurobiology, Meaning-Making, and the Escalation Continuum

Escalation does not begin with behavior. It begins with perception. Long before voices rise or boundaries are crossed, the nervous system has already evaluated the environment for safety or threat. This evaluation occurs automatically and is shaped by prior experience, current stressors, and the meanings assigned to interpersonal cues. Trauma-informed prevention requires understanding not only what people do, but how their brains and bodies interpret what is happening around them.

Neuroscience has established that the human stress response system reacts to psychological threat with the same biological intensity as physical danger[13]. When threat is perceived, the amygdala activates defensive neural circuits and triggers the hypothalamic–pituitary–adrenal (HPA) axis, releasing cortisol and adrenaline. Heart rate increases, muscles tense, and attention narrows. At the same time, activity in the prefrontal cortex decreases, impairing executive functioning, impulse control, empathy, and language processing[11,8]. In this state, behavior becomes governed by survival rather than reflection.

These physiological processes are not reserved for moments of crisis. They operate continuously in environments marked by chronic stress, uncertainty, and interpersonal tension. For individuals with histories of trauma or sustained adversity, the threshold for threat detection is often lower. What appears to be a minor interaction to one person may register as dangerous to another. Prevention begins with understanding how stress biology shapes perception and behavior long before visible escalation occurs.

Stress Biology and the Foundations of Escalation

Trauma reorganizes the brain around survival. Perry[1] demonstrated that repeated exposure to stress reshapes neural networks toward vigilance and reactivity. Van der Kolk[27] further showed that trauma is stored not only in narrative memory but in physiological patterns of arousal and emotional response. These patterns influence posture, tone of voice, and behavioral reactions long after the original threat has passed.

Chronic adversity produces measurable changes in brain structure and function. Neuroimaging studies document reductions in prefrontal cortex volume, enlargement of the amygdala, and alterations in hippocampal functioning among individuals exposed to sustained stress[12,11]. These changes impair executive functioning and heighten threat sensitivity.

Importantly, these stress-related adaptations appear across contexts. Similar neurobiological patterns are observed among individuals with high Adverse Childhood Experience scores, healthcare professionals experiencing burnout, and workers exposed to chronic organizational stress[13,21]. This common biology explains why prevention strategies grounded in regulation and relational safety are effective across education, healthcare, and workplace environments.

Understanding escalation as a biological process reframes prevention as physiological support rather than behavioral suppression. Professionals who remain calm, predictable, and respectful serve as external regulators for nervous systems operating under threat.

Adverse Childhood Experiences and Adverse Community Environments

The Adverse Childhood Experiences (ACE) study established a graded relationship between early adversity and lifelong physical and mental health outcomes[2]. Individuals exposed to four or more ACEs demonstrate significantly higher rates of depression, substance use, cardiovascular disease, and emotional dysregulation[20]. These findings revealed that childhood trauma is not an isolated psychological event but a public health issue with enduring neurological consequences.

Ellis and Dietz[28] expanded this framework through the concept of Adverse Community Environments, which include exposure to violence, discrimination, housing instability, environmental hazards, and chronic poverty. Ellis[6] describes ACEs and Adverse Community Environments as paired exposures—one rooted in early relational experience and the other in sustained environmental stress.

Together, these paired adversities shape how individuals experience authority, boundaries, and uncertainty. Chronic exposure to threat conditions the nervous system to anticipate danger. Hypervigilance becomes adaptive. Emotional reactivity becomes protective. What appears as aggression or withdrawal in institutional settings often reflects strategies learned in unsafe environments.

Research on trauma-informed school implementation has demonstrated that relational consistency and environmental supports significantly reduce disciplinary referrals and improve classroom climate, particularly in high-adversity communities[16]. These findings support the argument that prevention must address both personal history and environmental context.

Meaning-Making and Perception of Threat

Stress is not defined solely by events. It is defined by interpretation. Two individuals may experience the same interaction and respond very differently based on history, culture, and identity. Meaning-making lies at the center of escalation.

Trauma alters this interpretive lens, biasing perception toward danger[21]. Cultural background further shapes meaning. What one culture views as assertive, another may perceive as disrespectful[22]. Neurodivergence and sensory sensitivity add additional layers of complexity. Overstimulation may be mistaken for defiance. Communication differences may be misread as avoidance.

Armistead[23] found that pre-service teachers trained in trauma-informed interpretation were significantly more likely to respond to challenging behavior with curiosity rather than punishment. Prevention is therefore not merely a matter of technique but of perception.

Prevention requires slowing interpretation. It involves asking not only what happened, but what the interaction meant to the person experiencing it. This shift from certainty to curiosity represents one of the most powerful preventive interventions available.

Behavior as Communication

From a trauma-informed perspective, behavior communicates internal state long before it communicates intent. Refusal may signal fear or overwhelm. Anger may signal shame or loss of control. Withdrawal may signal exhaustion or hopelessness. These behaviors are not random. They are attempts to regulate distress.

When professionals interpret behavior as intentional misbehavior, they reinforce the perception of threat. When they interpret behavior as communication, they create space for regulation without abandoning boundaries. This shift does not eliminate accountability. It changes how accountability is delivered.

Desautels[29] emphasizes that discipline practices rooted in emotional co-regulation reduce escalation by restoring safety before behavioral correction is attempted. Behavioral science and trauma research converge on this principle: people escalate when they feel unsafe, unheard, or powerless.

Understood in this light, prevention focuses on restoring agency and dignity before a crisis emerges.

The Escalation Continuum

Escalation unfolds in recognizable stages. Prevention depends on identifying these stages early and responding in ways that restore regulation rather than intensify threat.

Table 1

The Escalation Continuum (Prevention Focus)

Stage	Internal State	Observable Cues	Prevention Opportunity
Baseline	Regulated	Calm posture, engagement	Relationship-building
Stress	Frustration, anxiety	Withdrawal, fidgeting	Validation, clarity
Agitation	Loss of control	Rigid thinking, pacing	Space, reduced demand

| Dysregulation | Survival dominant | Raised voice, refusal | Safety and containment |
| Crisis | Threat response | Aggression or shutdown | De-escalation required |

Prevention primarily occurs during the stress and agitation stages. Once a crisis is reached, prevention has already failed, and de-escalation becomes necessary. Recognizing early signs of escalation allows professionals to intervene before survival responses dominate behavior.

The escalation continuum reframes intervention as a temporal phenomenon. Timing matters as much as technique.

The Body as a Tool of Prevention

Prevention does not begin with language. It begins with presence. Nervous systems communicate continuously through posture, facial expression, movement, and tone of voice, often before conscious thought or verbal reasoning occurs. Research on nonverbal communication demonstrates that emotional meaning is transmitted through bodily cues before linguistic processing[30,31].

A calm posture slows physiological arousal. A rushed or abrupt tone increases it. Sudden movements signal danger. Steady breathing and relaxed facial expression communicate safety. In high-stress environments, professionals themselves become part of the regulatory environment. Their bodies function as cues of stability or threat, shaping how others interpret the situation before any words are spoken.

From a neurobiological perspective, this process is mediated through the autonomic nervous system. Polyvagal theory describes how facial expression, vocal prosody, and posture activate either defensive circuits or the social engagement system8. When cues signal safety, neural pathways associated with connection and regulation become accessible. When cues signal threat, defensive responses dominate, and cognitive flexibility diminishes.

Self-regulation thus becomes prevention. Professionals who understand their own physiological responses—tightened muscles, accelerated breathing, rising vocal pitch—can interrupt escalation before it spreads relationally. The ability to notice and modulate one's bodily state is not ancillary to prevention; it is foundational.

Prevention-oriented practice begins with somatic awareness. Training that neglects bodily presence in favor of verbal techniques alone overlooks the most immediate channel through which safety or threat is communicated. In trauma-informed systems, regulation is transmitted not only through policy and language, but through embodied interaction.

Emotional Regulation as Neurobiological Training

Emotional regulation is often misunderstood as self-control or emotional suppression. In trauma-informed neuroscience, regulation is not defined by the absence of emotion but by the capacity to return the nervous system to safety following activation. This distinction is foundational to prevention. Suppression requires cognitive force. Regulation requires neural learning.

When individuals are triggered, the amygdala initiates threat circuitry while the prefrontal cortex temporarily loses regulatory influence[11,8]. In this state, reasoning, empathy, and language processing are impaired. No amount of instruction or discipline can restore regulation from within the survival brain alone. Regulation must be learned through repeated experiences of safety rather than imposed through punishment.

Neuroplasticity provides the biological mechanism for prevention. Each time an individual notices activation, pauses, and returns to equilibrium, neural pathways associated with calm and cognitive flexibility are strengthened[24,14]. Over time, these pathways become default responses under stress. This process is neither instantaneous nor linear. It requires consistent relational and environmental reinforcement.

Emotionally intelligent behavior is subsequently not a personality trait but a trained capacity. Individuals who appear calm under pressure are not immune to stress. They have practiced regulation repeatedly in environments that supported recovery rather than shame. Leadership, parenting, and professional conduct all shape neural expectations. What is practiced becomes patterned. What is patterned becomes automatic.

Armistead's[23] research on trauma-informed pre-service teacher training demonstrates that educators who learn regulation strategies grounded in neurodevelopmental principles show significantly greater capacity to respond calmly and proportionally to challenging classroom behavior. These findings support the conclusion that prevention can be taught and that emotional regulation is an educational outcome rather than an inherent disposition.

This reconceptualization shifts prevention away from behavioral compliance toward capacity building. Regulation is not something individuals either possess or lack; it is something environments cultivate. Systems that consistently respond to stress with predictability, dignity, and relational safety strengthen regulatory circuits across time.

Neuroplasticity and Prevention

Neuroplasticity explains why early intervention matters and why relational environments are powerful. The brain adapts to patterns of interaction. Environments that provide predictable safety strengthen regulatory circuits. Environments characterized by unpredictability and humiliation strengthen threat circuits.

Siegel[24] describes this process as "experience-dependent wiring." When individuals experience attuned relationships, their nervous systems learn to associate stress with recovery rather than collapse. Over time, this learning generalizes across contexts.

Mindfulness-based and relational interventions demonstrate measurable changes in brain structure and function. Studies show increased prefrontal cortex thickness and decreased amygdala reactivity following sustained regulation practice[32,33]. These findings confirm that emotional regulation can be cultivated intentionally rather than assumed as a fixed trait.

From a prevention perspective, this means that everyday interactions matter. A calm voice, respectful correction, and consistent routines all serve as neurological training tools. Over time, they reduce the likelihood that stress will escalate into a crisis.

ACEs, Community Stress, and the Regulation Threshold

Individuals with high ACE exposure and those living in Adverse Community Environments often operate with a lowered regulation threshold. Their nervous systems have learned that danger is frequent and unpredictable. Hypervigilance becomes adaptive. Emotional reactivity becomes protective.

Ellis[6] argues that ACEs and Adverse Community Environments must be understood as paired exposures. One shapes internal regulation capacity; the other sustains external stress. Together, they increase vulnerability to escalation in institutional settings.

Trauma-informed prevention models have demonstrated measurable reductions in behavioral incidents in schools serving high-adversity communities[16]. These results suggest that regulation capacity can be strengthened even when environmental stress remains high.

For this reason, prevention requires designing systems that compensate for chronic stress rather than amplifying it. Predictability, relational continuity, and dignity-centered communication act as stabilizers for nervous systems shaped by adversity.

Co-Regulation as the Bridge to Self-Regulation

Regulation does not develop in isolation. It is learned relationally. Polyvagal theory describes the social engagement system as a biological mechanism through which safety is communicated via facial expression, vocal tone, and posture[8]. When these cues convey calm, they activate neural circuits associated with connection rather than defense.

Desautels[29] emphasizes that discipline practices rooted in emotional co-regulation reduce escalation by restoring emotional safety before behavioral correction is attempted. When adults remain regulated in the presence of distress, they function as external regulators for developing or overwhelmed nervous systems. This relational stabilization allows the individual to re-engage prefrontal functioning and regain agency.

Co-regulation does not eliminate boundaries. It transforms how boundaries are experienced. A boundary delivered through anger communicates threat. A boundary delivered through calm communicates containment. Over time, repeated experiences of co-regulation teach the nervous system that stress does not require collapse or aggression.

Crnobori's[16] findings further demonstrate that relational consistency combined with environmental supports such as regulation spaces and structured transitions leads to significant reductions in disciplinary referrals. These outcomes reflect neurological stabilization rather than behavioral compliance.

From a systems perspective, co-regulation must be modeled and supported organizationally. Professionals cannot consistently regulate others in environments that disregard their own stress. Reflective supervision, peer support, and leadership modeling function as higher-order co-regulation structures that stabilize entire systems.

Dignity, Shame, and Threat Perception

Shame is one of the most powerful accelerators of escalation. Neurobiological research demonstrates that experiences of humiliation, rejection, and public correction activate neural circuits associated with physical danger and social pain[27,34]. When dignity is compromised, the nervous system interprets the experience as a threat to belonging and survival, triggering defensive responses.

Dignity functions as a protective factor. When individuals feel respected, their nervous systems remain accessible to reasoning and reflection. When dignity is violated, defensive behavior emerges rapidly. This dynamic explains why public reprimands frequently escalate situations that private, respectful conversations resolve.

Prevention therefore requires attention not only to what boundaries are set, but to how they are delivered. Discipline that preserves dignity communicates that limits exist within a relationship. Discipline that induces shame communicates exclusion. The difference is not merely interpersonal. It is biological.

Social neuroscience confirms that social rejection activates the same brain regions involved in physical pain[34]. These findings underscore both the ethical and practical necessity of dignity-centered responses. In trauma-informed systems, correction must occur without humiliation, and accountability must be paired with relational safety.

When organizations normalize shame-based practices—public criticism, zero-tolerance responses, or deficit-focused documentation—they unintentionally reinforce threat circuitry. Conversely, systems that prioritize dignity cultivate psychological safety and preserve access to executive functioning during moments of stress.

Micro-Escalations and the Early Warning System

Escalation rarely occurs without precursors. It unfolds through subtle physiological and behavioral cues known as micro-escalations: changes in posture, narrowed attention, increased pacing, shallow breathing, reduced verbal flexibility, or withdrawal from engagement. These signals reflect rising stress and diminishing regulatory capacity.

Professionals trained to recognize these cues gain access to early prevention points. A simple acknowledgment of frustration, a reduction in demand, or a brief pause in interaction can restore regulation. When these cues are ignored, stress accumulates until survival responses dominate.

Crnobori's[16] trauma-informed school implementation work emphasized that structured recognition of early stress signals significantly reduced disciplinary incidents by creating intervention opportunities before crisis emerged. These findings reinforce that prevention is temporal. Timing matters as much as technique.

Micro-escalations function as a neural warning system. Prevention depends on responding to these cues with curiosity rather than correction and with regulation rather than authority.

Communication that Regulates the Nervous System

Communication is not neutral. It shapes emotional state through rhythm, tone, and meaning. Language can escalate or stabilize. Prevention-oriented communication is characterized by clarity, empathy, and proportionality.

Active listening communicates safety. It signals that the individual's internal state has been registered. This recognition alone can reduce physiological arousal and restore access to reflective thought. Empathic statements do not excuse harmful behavior. They acknowledge emotional experience while maintaining boundaries.

Tone matters more than content during stress. A calm tone activates the social engagement system. A harsh or abrupt tone activates threat responses. Prevention therefore requires conscious modulation of voice, facial expression, and pacing.

Miscommunication is one of the most common escalation triggers. Digital communication amplifies this risk by removing nonverbal cues. Treviño et al.[7] found that ambiguity and power differentials in electronic communication increase emotional reactivity.

Prevention-oriented systems establish norms that prioritize clarity, relational contact, and opportunities for repair when misinterpretation occurs.

Table 2

Communication as Neurobiological Intervention

Communication Feature	Neural Impact	Escalation Risk
Calm tone	Activates social engagement	Low
Abrupt commands	Activates threat response	High
Validation	Restores prefrontal access	Low
Public correction	Triggers shame	High
Repair	Rebuilds trust	Low

Language functions as a regulatory tool. It shapes whether individuals experience interactions as safe or threatening. Communication that preserves dignity and acknowledges emotion strengthens regulatory circuits. Communication that shames or commands narrows cognitive access and increases defensive behavior

Classroom and Organizational Applications

Trauma-informed prevention strategies apply across settings. In classrooms, regulation spaces, predictable routines, and relational check-ins reduce baseline stress and improve engagement. Armistead[23] found that trauma-informed classroom environments strengthened both academic participation and emotional regulation among students.

In healthcare and workplace settings, similar principles apply. Predictable schedules, respectful communication, and reflective supervision reduce burnout and emotional volatility[35]. These interventions do not eliminate stress; they change how stress is metabolized.

Prevention also requires acknowledging the impact of Adverse Community Environments. Organizations serving high-adversity populations must avoid replicating external stressors through rigid policies or punitive practices. Instead, they can function as buffers against instability by providing consistency, dignity, and relational safety.

Across sectors, trauma-informed prevention shifts focus from rule enforcement to relational design. It asks how systems can structure daily interactions to support regulation rather than intensify threat. Environmental design, leadership practices, and communication norms all function as prevention tools.

Integration of Neuroscience and Systems

Neuroscience and systems theory converge on a single conclusion: escalation is predictable and preventable when early signals are recognized and environments support regulation. Individual skill without systemic support is fragile. Systemic design without relational skill is hollow. Prevention emerges when both operate in alignment.

Emotional regulation is a trained capacity.

Co-regulation is its foundation.

Communication is its vehicle.

Dignity is its ethic.

Environment is its amplifier.

Understanding escalation as a neurobiological and relational process shifts prevention from crisis management to capacity building. It transforms everyday interactions into opportunities for neurological training rather than moments of correction.

When organizations design environments that support regulation, they reduce the frequency and intensity of crises. When leaders model calm under pressure, they teach the organization's nervous system what to expect. Over time, these patterns become culture.

Prevention is not the absence of adversity. It is the presence of systems that teach the brain how to return to safety.

The next chapter examines how organizational culture, leadership, and environmental design can institutionalize these principles, transforming individual regulation into systemic prevention.

Chapter 4

Designing Prevention-Oriented Systems

Culture, Leadership, and Environmental Regulation

If escalation is rooted in neurobiology and meaning-making, then prevention must be embedded in the environments that shape those processes. Individual skill alone cannot counteract systems that amplify threat, confusion, or inequity. Organizations themselves function as emotional regulators. Their policies, routines, leadership practices, and physical spaces communicate whether individuals are safe, valued, and heard. Prevention, thus, becomes a property of design rather than a reaction to crisis.

Trauma-informed research has consistently demonstrated that environments exert a powerful influence on emotional regulation and behavioral outcomes[26,21]. Individuals do not enter schools, hospitals, or workplaces as isolated nervous systems. They bring with them histories of adversity, community stress, and prior experiences with authority. These histories interact with organizational structures to produce either stabilization or threat. Prevention depends not only on how professionals respond in moments of stress, but on what institutions signal every day through their culture and practices.

A prevention-oriented system is not defined by the absence of conflict. It is defined by the presence of conditions that reduce the likelihood that stress will evolve into escalation. These conditions include predictability, relational continuity, fairness, and opportunities for agency. When such conditions are embedded in organizational life, they operate as silent regulators, shaping behavior long before a crisis emerges.

Culture as a Regulatory System

Organizational culture functions as an emotional ecosystem. It communicates what is valued, what is feared, and what is permissible. Culture influences how individuals interpret behavior, how mistakes are addressed, and how conflict is managed. In high-stress environments, culture often develops under pressure and is shaped by crisis rather than intention.

Trauma-informed theory emphasizes that cultures characterized by blame, secrecy, and rigid hierarchy mirror the dynamics of traumatic environments[37]. These cultures increase threat perception and reduce psychological safety. Conversely, cultures characterized by transparency, collaboration, and learning promote regulation and trust. Edmondson's[36] research on psychological safety demonstrates that teams function more effectively when members feel safe to express concerns without fear of humiliation or punishment.

Cultural norms shape whether behavior is interpreted as communication or defiance. In punitive cultures, deviation is viewed as a challenge to authority. In prevention-oriented cultures, deviation is viewed as information about stress, misunderstanding, or unmet needs. This distinction profoundly alters professional response and individual experience of power.

Culture also determines how mistakes are understood. When mistakes are framed as moral failures, shame and defensiveness follow. When mistakes are framed as learning opportunities, curiosity and accountability emerge. Prevention depends on narratives that normalize struggle while maintaining boundaries.

Leadership as Emotional Architecture

Leadership functions as emotional architecture within organizations. Leaders model how stress is interpreted and how conflict is handled. Their responses to pressure shape the nervous system of the entire system. When leaders respond with volatility or blame, they normalize reactivity. When leaders respond with steadiness and inquiry, they normalize regulation.

Trauma-informed leadership emphasizes consistency, transparency, and proportionality[26]. Consistency reduces uncertainty, which in turn reduces threat perception. Transparency reduces rumors and suspicion. Proportionality ensures that responses match the level of concern rather than amplifying it unnecessarily.

Leaders also determine whether prevention becomes embedded or remains aspirational. Policies may articulate values, but daily behavior enacts them. When leaders prioritize relational safety alongside performance, they signal that emotional well-being is not secondary to productivity.

Leadership practices that emphasize listening, shared problem-solving, and reflective supervision create conditions for co-regulation across the organization. Over time, these practices shape a culture in which escalation is less likely because the threat is addressed early and respectfully.

Environmental Design and Predictability

Physical and organizational environments influence the regulation of the nervous system. Predictable routines, clear signage, and coherent spatial design reduce cognitive load and increase perceived safety. In contrast, chaotic environments marked by noise, crowding, and ambiguity amplify stress responses.

Environmental design has been recognized as a core component of trauma-informed care. Hospitals that modify lighting, waiting room layout, and privacy protocols report reductions in patient distress and staff conflict[38]. Schools that implement regulation spaces and structured transitions observe fewer behavioral incidents and improved climate[16].

Predictability functions as a biological stabilizer. When individuals can anticipate what will happen next, their nervous systems remain closer to baseline. When environments are unpredictable, hypervigilance increases.

Environmental design also includes symbolic elements. Messages displayed on walls, language used in forms, and tone of announcements all contribute to meaning-making. Environments that emphasize rules without relationship communicate threat. Environments that emphasize belonging communicate safety.

Adverse Community Environments and Institutional Responsibility

Ellis[6] argues that Adverse Childhood Experiences must be understood in tandem with Adverse Community Environments, including exposure to violence, discrimination, housing instability, and chronic poverty. Institutions serving such communities operate within layers of stress that extend beyond individual history.

When organizations fail to account for these conditions, they risk interpreting stress-driven behavior as moral failure rather than adaptive response. Prevention requires institutional humility, the recognition that behavior reflects broader social forces. This recognition does not excuse harm but contextualizes it.

Institutions therefore bear responsibility for designing responses that buffer rather than amplify community stress. This includes equitable policy enforcement, culturally responsive communication, and partnerships with community resources.

Prevention becomes a shared societal project rather than an individual burden.

Communication Systems as Prevention Structures

Communication systems are among the most powerful determinants of emotional climate. Policies, emails, announcements, and meetings all function as regulatory signals. Tone and clarity influence whether individuals feel respected or controlled.

Prevention-oriented communication systems emphasize clarity, empathy, and opportunities for dialogue. They reduce ambiguity and provide pathways for feedback and repair. In contrast, communication systems that rely on command and compliance increase defensiveness and mistrust.

Digital communication presents particular challenges. The absence of nonverbal cues increases the risk of misinterpretation. Treviño et al.[7] found that ambiguity in digital messages heightens emotional reactivity, particularly in environments characterized by power differentials. Prevention-oriented systems consequently establish norms that prioritize relational contact for emotionally charged issues.

Communication systems also shape institutional narratives. When conflict is framed as failure, shame increases. When conflict is framed as information, learning becomes possible. Over time, these narratives determine whether escalation becomes chronic or rare.

Table 1

Environmental Features That Influence Escalation Risk

Feature	Escalation-Oriented System	Prevention-Oriented System
Rules	Inconsistent, punitive	Clear, fair, predictable
Space	Crowded, chaotic	Organized, calming
Communication	Abrupt, impersonal	Respectful, relational
Leadership	Reactive, authoritarian	Reflective, transparent
Culture	Blame-based	Learning-oriented

Policy Coherence and Ethical Alignment

Prevention requires alignment between values, training, and policy. When organizations teach trauma-informed principles but enforce zero-tolerance policies, contradiction emerges. Professionals are placed in impossible positions, expected to demonstrate empathy while administering punishment. These contradictions undermine prevention and erode trust.

Policy coherence means that rules reflect the same dignity-centered philosophy promoted in training. Accountability is paired with opportunity for repair. Documentation systems capture context rather than only violations.

Aligned systems reduce ambiguity. When expectations are shared and responses are consistent, individuals experience less threat.

This consistency becomes a regulatory force, stabilizing interactions across roles and settings.

Ethical prevention asks whether institutional practices create safety or fear, whether they reduce harm or reproduce it, and whether they invite understanding or enforce silence. These questions ground prevention in values rather than convenience.

Environmental Design as a Prevention Strategy: Biophilic and Trauma-Informed Spaces

If escalation is shaped by neurobiology and meaning-making, then physical space becomes a form of communication. Walls, lighting, sound, temperature, and layout all signal whether an environment is safe, threatening, predictable, or chaotic. Environmental design is not neutral. It exerts regulatory influence on the nervous system and serves as a silent participant in every interaction.

Trauma-informed and biophilic design frameworks converge on a central insight: environments that support sensory regulation reduce stress and improve emotional stability. The Biophilic Design Assessment[15] emphasizes that access to natural light, greenery, airflow, and visual complexity drawn from nature lowers physiological arousal and supports cognitive functioning. These effects are mediated through reductions in cortisol, improved attention restoration, and increased parasympathetic nervous system activity.

For individuals with histories of Adverse Childhood Experiences or those living in Adverse Community Environments, environmental cues are particularly salient. Chronic exposure to danger conditions the nervous system to scan for threat. Environments that are noisy, crowded, poorly lit, or unpredictable reinforce this vigilance. In contrast, environments designed with refuge, coherence, and sensory balance communicate safety before any human interaction occurs.

Biophilic design principles include:

- access to natural light
- visual connection to plants or outdoor views
- use of natural materials and textures
- spaces that balance openness with refuge
- predictable spatial organization
- reduction of harsh sensory input

These features reduce cognitive load and support emotional regulation. In schools, they contribute to improved attention and reduced behavioral incidents. In healthcare settings, they reduce patient anxiety and staff burnout. In workplaces, they support sustained concentration and emotional steadiness. Across contexts, they function as preventive infrastructure.

Environmental design also carries symbolic meaning. A space that feels cared for communicates that the people within it are valued. A space that feels neglected communicates disregard. This symbolism shapes identity and belonging, both of which are central to prevention.

Sensory Regulation and the Nervous System

The nervous system continuously interprets sensory input as safe or threatening. Loud noises, flickering lights, and overcrowded hallways activate threat responses even when no interpersonal conflict exists. For individuals already operating near their stress threshold, such inputs can push the system into dysregulation.

Trauma-informed environmental design prioritizes sensory modulation. This includes:

- quiet zones for recovery
- softer lighting
- reduced visual clutter
- clear wayfinding
- access to movement
- opportunities for solitude

These features function as upstream prevention by lowering baseline arousal. Rather than relying on behavioral intervention after stress has accumulated, the environment itself becomes a regulator.

Biophilic Design highlights that environments incorporating natural patterns and elements promote attention restoration and emotional balance. These effects are not aesthetic luxuries. They are physiological supports[15]. Prevention, in this sense, begins with architecture.

In schools, this may take the form of calming corners or outdoor learning spaces. In healthcare, it may involve patient rooms with windows and quiet waiting areas. In workplaces, it may include flexible workspaces that allow for movement and privacy. The principle is the same: environments should reduce threat and increase choice.

Environmental Predictability and Cognitive Load

Unpredictability is a primary driver of stress. When individuals cannot anticipate what will happen next, the brain remains in a state of vigilance. Prevention-oriented systems therefore emphasize environmental predictability. This includes consistent schedules, clear signage, and stable routines.

Spatial predictability reduces cognitive burden. Individuals who know where to go and what to expect conserve mental energy for learning and problem-solving. This is especially important for those with trauma histories, neurodivergence, or sensory sensitivities.

Predictability also extends to social environments. Regular seating arrangements, consistent meeting formats, and transparent procedures create psychological safety. These practices align with biophilic design's emphasis on coherence and pattern.

Environmental predictability does not imply rigidity. It provides a stable framework within which flexibility can occur. This balance mirrors the nervous system's need for both structure and autonomy.

Environment as Nonverbal Communication

Every environment tells a story. A hallway lined with surveillance cameras communicates control. A hallway lined with student artwork communicates belonging. A waiting room with harsh lighting communicates efficiency. A waiting room with plants and comfortable seating communicates care.

These messages influence behavior long before verbal interaction begins. When individuals enter a space that feels hostile or sterile, their nervous systems prepare for defense. When they enter a space that feels welcoming, their nervous systems prepare for connection.

Environmental communication is particularly important in high-stress systems where individuals may already feel marginalized or unsafe. For communities affected by Adverse Community Environments, institutions often represent authority and judgment.

Thoughtful environmental design can counteract these associations by signaling dignity and respect.

The Biophilic Design framework reinforces that nature-based elements foster a sense of continuity and grounding. These cues are especially powerful for individuals who have experienced chaos or displacement. They offer a visual and sensory reminder of stability[15].

Equity and Access in Environmental Prevention

Prevention through design must be equitable. Historically, calming and supportive environments have been reserved for privileged spaces, while under-resourced communities experience overcrowded, deteriorating facilities. This disparity reinforces stress and behavioral risk.

Ellis[6] emphasizes that Adverse Community Environments shape emotional regulation across the lifespan. Institutions serving these communities carry a responsibility to counterbalance environmental stress rather than replicate it. Biophilic and trauma-informed design principles should not be luxuries but standards.

Equitable prevention design includes:

- access to natural light in all spaces
- safe and clean facilities
- quiet areas for regulation
- inclusive design for neurodiversity
- culturally affirming visuals and symbols

These features communicate belonging and safety rather than surveillance and control.

Environmental justice is subsequently inseparable from prevention. When institutions invest in supportive spaces, they invest in nervous system regulation at a population level.

Integration with Leadership and Culture

Environmental design does not operate in isolation. It interacts with leadership behavior and organizational culture. A calming space loses meaning if leadership communicates fear and urgency. Conversely, supportive leadership is undermined by chaotic environments.

Prevention-oriented systems align:

- physical space
- communication norms
- leadership practices
- policy coherence

When these elements are consistent, individuals experience safety across multiple levels. When they conflict, confusion and mistrust emerge.

Leaders influence how spaces are used. A regulation room becomes punitive if used for exclusion. It becomes preventive if used for restoration. The same environment can serve different purposes depending on organizational meaning.

Thus, environmental design must be accompanied by training and shared language. Professionals must understand why these spaces exist and how they support regulation rather than control.

Table 2

Environmental Design as Prevention

Feature	Threat-Oriented Environment	Prevention-Oriented Environment
Lighting	Harsh, artificial	Natural, adjustable
Sound	Loud, echoing	Buffered, quiet zones
Layout	Crowded, confusing	Predictable, clear
Visuals	Surveillance-focused	Belonging-focused
Nature	Absent	Integrated
Choice	Restricted	Flexible

Relational Continuity and Staffing Models

Environmental prevention is strengthened by relational continuity. Stable staffing patterns reduce uncertainty and support trust. When individuals encounter consistent professionals, their nervous systems require less energy to assess safety.

High turnover and rotating supervision increase stress and undermine prevention. In contrast, systems that prioritize long-term relationships foster emotional stability. This principle applies in schools, healthcare, and workplaces alike.

Relational continuity also supports staff regulation. Professionals who feel known and supported are better able to regulate others.

This reciprocal process creates a culture of co-regulation rather than control.

Reflective Supervision as Prevention Infrastructure

Supervision functions as an internal environment. Reflective supervision provides space for professionals to process emotional experiences and examine interpretive habits. It shifts focus from compliance to meaning-making.

When supervision emphasizes curiosity and learning, professionals develop a greater capacity to respond calmly to stress. When supervision emphasizes blame, professionals become defensive and rigid. Prevention depends on supervisory culture.

Reflective supervision reinforces the same principles as biophilic design: safety, predictability, and connection. It provides an emotional refuge within organizational structure.

Communication Systems and Environmental Meaning

Communication systems operate alongside physical environments. Emails, announcements, and policies shape emotional climate. Prevention-oriented communication emphasizes clarity, respect, and opportunities for dialogue.

Digital communication must be used thoughtfully. Ambiguous messages increase stress, particularly in hierarchical systems. Prevention requires matching the medium to the message and prioritizing relational contact for emotionally charged issues.

Communication also constructs meaning about space. A regulation room can be described as a place for recovery or a place for punishment. The words chosen determine how it is experienced.

Integration and Synthesis

Designing prevention-oriented systems requires alignment between neuroscience, environment, culture, and leadership. Physical spaces regulate nervous systems. Communication regulates meaning. Leadership regulates emotional climate. Policies regulate expectations.

Together, these elements create either escalation-prone or prevention-oriented systems. Prevention is not a single intervention. It is a pattern of design choices that support regulation before crisis emerges.

Environmental design, particularly through biophilic and trauma-informed principles, offers a powerful yet underutilized prevention strategy. By shaping sensory experience, institutions shape behavior. By shaping meaning, they shape belonging.

The next chapter will move from prevention to de-escalation, examining what happens when stress exceeds regulatory capacity and crisis emerges. De-escalation builds upon the same principles of safety, dignity, and relational regulation, applying them when prevention is no longer sufficient.

Communication as a Preventive Tool

When stress begins to rise, communication becomes the primary regulatory tool. How information is conveyed can either stabilize or accelerate escalation. Clarity, tone, pacing, and body language work together to signal safety or threat.

Effective early intervention communication prioritizes:

- Accurate reflection over persuasion
- Validation without endorsement

- Boundaries without humiliation
- Calm presence over urgency

Stephen Porges' polyvagal theory reminds us that individuals unconsciously scan for cues of safety through voice, facial expression, and posture[8]. A regulated professional can interrupt escalation simply by slowing the interaction and reducing perceived threat.

Bias Awareness and Interpretive Pauses

Under stress, human beings rely on cognitive shortcuts. These shortcuts increase the risk of misinterpretation, particularly across lines of race, culture, disability, and authority. Trauma-informed early intervention requires intentional pauses to examine assumptions before responding.

An interpretive pause allows professionals to ask:

- What else might be driving this behavior?
- What stressors may be invisible to me?
- Am I reacting to behavior, or responding to threat?

Bias-aware prevention does not eliminate accountability. It improves accuracy. By reducing misattribution, systems reduce unnecessary escalation and inequitable outcomes.

Supervisory Interventions: Coaching and Mediation

Supervisors play a critical role in early intervention. When tension emerges between staff members, or between staff and clients, timely support can prevent conflict from becoming entrenched.

Trauma-informed supervisory tools include:

- Conflict coaching focused on perspective-taking
- Facilitated conversations emphasizing safety and repair
- Clear role clarification and expectation setting
- Supportive feedback delivered without shame

When supervisors intervene early and neutrally, they reinforce a culture where concerns are addressed before formal grievance or disciplinary processes are triggered.

Bystander Intervention and Shared Responsibility

Prevention is not the responsibility of a single role. Trauma-informed systems train all staff to engage in respectful bystander intervention when they observe rising stress or unsafe dynamics.

Bystander strategies may include grounding prompts, supportive redirection, or discreet offers of relief. These interventions are most effective when they are normalized through training and modeled by leadership.

Shared responsibility distributes emotional labor and reduces isolation — both protective factors against burnout and escalation.

Integrating Early Intervention into Policy and Training

For early intervention to be sustainable, it must be embedded into organizational systems rather than left to individual discretion. Policies, procedures, and training programs should explicitly reinforce preventive action.

Key elements include:

- Clear pathways for informal resolution
- Protection against retaliation for raising concerns

- Regular skill-based training with practice opportunities
- Documentation processes that capture early signals, not just incidents
- When early intervention is operationalized, organizations reduce crisis frequency and strengthen trust.

Preventing Escalation in the Moment: Attunement and Early Regulation

Prevention does not end with environmental design or organizational policy. It also unfolds in real time, within everyday human interactions. Long before anger, shutdown, or crisis emerges, the nervous system communicates rising stress through subtle and often nonverbal signals. These early indicators—changes in posture, tone, pacing, facial expression, or engagement—represent a critical window for prevention.

At this stage, individuals have not yet lost access to executive functioning. They may feel anxious, frustrated, confused, or overwhelmed, but they remain capable of processing language, making meaning, and responding to relational cues. Prevention in this moment depends on attunement: the capacity to notice emerging tension and respond in ways that restore safety before dysregulation occurs.

This form of prevention is not crisis intervention. It is relational regulation. It operates through presence, curiosity, and embodied communication rather than authority or correction. In this sense, prevention becomes a dance of nervous systems, in which one regulated individual can help stabilize another simply by how they enter the interaction.

Recognizing Early Signals of Stress

Escalation rarely appears without warning. Early signs of rising stress may include:

- shallow or rapid breathing
- tightened posture or rigid movements
- avoidance of eye contact
- changes in tone or speech rate
- withdrawal or silence
- increased fidgeting or pacing
- narrowed attention or repetitive thinking

These signals do not yet indicate crisis. They indicate vulnerability. When professionals are trained to recognize these cues, they gain access to prevention points that occur before threat responses dominate behavior.

Rather than interpreting these signs as defiance or resistance, a prevention-oriented stance treats them as information about internal state. The question shifts from "How do I correct this?" to "What might this person be experiencing right now?"

Self-Regulation as the First Preventive Act

Prevention in the moment begins not with the other person, but with oneself. Professionals bring their own nervous systems into every interaction. Tone of voice, posture, and pacing communicate safety or threat long before words are processed.

A rushed response increases arousal. A calm response reduces it. A defensive posture signals danger. A grounded posture signals containment.

Before intervening verbally, a prevention-oriented professional pauses to notice their own physiological state:

Is my voice tightening?

Is my body leaning forward aggressively?

Am I feeling hurried or threatened?

Am I reacting or responding?

This self-check is not passive. It is active regulation. By stabilizing their own nervous system, professionals prevent escalation from spreading relationally. In this way, self-regulation becomes a form of prevention rather than merely a personal skill.

Attunement Through Curiosity and Care

Attunement communicates safety through interest rather than authority. It signals that the individual is seen rather than judged. Even brief expressions of care can interrupt escalation trajectories when offered early.

Simple, relational inquiries such as:

- "You seem tense—how can I help right now?"
- "Is something making this harder than it needs to be?"
- "Do you need a moment before we continue?"
- "I want to understand what's going on for you."

These statements do not excuse harmful behavior. They acknowledge emotional experience while maintaining relational connection. They slow the interaction, widen cognitive space, and allow the nervous system to settle before survival responses take over.

This approach resembles the best practices of customer service, not because it is superficial, but because it recognizes that people escalate when they feel unseen, rushed, or powerless. Curiosity restores agency. Care restores dignity. Together, they function as preventive regulation.

The Body as a Signal of Safety

Attunement is conveyed as much through the body as through language. A softened posture, slower movements, and a steady voice communicate reassurance without requiring explanation. These signals activate the social engagement system and reduce perceived threat.

In many cases, prevention occurs without words at all:

- stepping back to give physical space
- lowering one's voice
- sitting rather than standing over
- allowing silence
- maintaining relaxed facial expression

These embodied actions tell the nervous system: You are safe. You are not being attacked. You are not alone in this moment.

This is especially important when there is no prior relationship. Prevention does not require history; it requires presence. Even first encounters can stabilize stress when the interaction communicates respect and calm rather than urgency or control.

Preventing Escalation Without Taking Control

A central feature of prevention is that it does not seize authority prematurely. It does not impose solutions or rush to correct behavior. Instead, it preserves agency while offering support.

Key principles of interactional prevention include:

- slowing the pace rather than increasing it
- asking rather than telling
- listening rather than diagnosing
- signaling safety rather than enforcing compliance
- responding to tension rather than reacting to behavior

This approach keeps the individual within a regulated zone. Once anger, shouting, or shutdown occurs, de-escalation becomes necessary. But when stress is still rising and cognition remains accessible, prevention remains possible.

A Continuum of Prevention

This form of early, interactional prevention exists alongside environmental and organizational prevention. It bridges system design and individual encounter.

Environmental prevention shapes baseline stress.
Interactional prevention stabilizes rising tension.
De-escalation responds when regulation has already been lost.

Together, they form a continuum rather than separate categories.

Prevention, in this sense, is not the absence of conflict. It is the presence of awareness, attunement, and care at the earliest signs of strain.

Closing Integration

Preventing escalation in the moment requires noticing what others often overlook: subtle signals of distress, shifts in tone, changes in posture, and the quiet signs of anxiety or overwhelm. It also requires humility—the willingness to examine one's own impact on the interaction and to choose curiosity over certainty.

When professionals slow interactions, regulate their own bodies, and communicate care before crisis emerges, they transform ordinary moments into opportunities for stabilization. These small acts accumulate. Over time, they reduce the frequency of escalation and strengthen relational trust.

This is not de-escalation. It is the prevention of escalation.

It is the art of sensing tension and guiding it back toward safety before survival takes over.

SECTION 2:

DE-ESCALATION

Chapter 5

Understanding the Nature of Escalation

The psychological, emotional, and behavioral patterns of conflict escalation

Escalation as a Neurobiological and Relational Process

Before conflict can be interrupted, it must be understood. Escalation is often described as a breakdown in behavior or communication, but this framing is incomplete. Escalation is not merely an interpersonal failure; it is a predictable neurobiological and relational process shaped by perceived threat, meaning-making, and environmental context.

Escalation does not begin with shouting or visible confrontation. It begins internally—with tightened muscles, shallow breathing, and the silent accumulation of stress between what an individual needs and what they believe they are receiving. It is the friction between emotion and expression, frequently invisible until it becomes unmistakable. These early physiological and psychological shifts signal that the nervous system is moving away from safety and toward survival.

Across healthcare, education, and human services research, escalation is increasingly understood as a patterned response to perceived threat rather than willful misconduct[40,39]. This reframing moves professionals away from moral judgment and toward interpretation. Instead of asking, "Why is this person behaving this way?" the more accurate question becomes, "What is happening in this person's nervous system right now?"

Neurobiologically, escalation reflects a shift in brain functioning. When a threat is perceived, the amygdala activates survival circuitry, and the prefrontal cortex becomes less accessible. Cognitive flexibility narrows, emotional reactivity increases, and the capacity for language, perspective-taking, and problem-solving diminishes[41,42]. In this state, individuals are not choosing their reactions through logic; they are responding through protective reflex.

Escalation is also relational. Human nervous systems do not operate in isolation. They continuously read and respond to cues from others, including their tone of voice, facial expressions, posture, and proximity. A raised voice, a rigid stance, or a dismissive response can amplify threat, while calm presence and respectful communication can reduce it. Conflict, in turn, unfolds between nervous systems as much as between people.

This relational dimension explains why the same stressor may produce different outcomes depending on context. A firm directive from a trusted supervisor may feel containing, while the same words from an unfamiliar authority figure may feel controlling or dangerous. Meaning is shaped not only by what happens, but by who delivers it and how.

Understanding escalation requires attention to both internal and external forces. Trauma histories, unmet needs, power dynamics, and organizational culture all influence how threat is perceived and how stress is expressed. What appears to be defiance, withdrawal, or hostility may reflect fear, overload, or loss of control. Without this lens, professionals risk responding to behavior while missing its origin.

Equally important is recognizing one's own participation in escalation. This chapter is not only about identifying when others are escalating. It is also about noticing when one's own nervous system is activated. Professionals under stress are vulnerable to the same biological shifts: narrowed attention, urgency, and reactivity. Escalation often becomes mutual before it becomes visible.

Understanding escalation allows professionals to make better choices under pressure, avoid unintentional harm, and shift from reacting to responding. This shift—from reflex to reflection—forms the conceptual foundation of de-escalation[43,44,45]. When escalation is seen as a process rather than a personal failure, intervention becomes possible earlier, safer, and more humane.

This chapter will explore how escalation unfolds across physiological, psychological, and organizational levels. By examining the escalation cycle, nervous system responses, trauma influences, and environmental conditions, professionals gain a framework for recognizing stress before it becomes a crisis and for responding with clarity rather than control.

The Escalation Cycle: Triggers, Peaks, and Resolution

Conflict rarely erupts without warning. It builds along a pathway that can be anticipated, observed, and sometimes redirected. The behavioral crisis literature demonstrates that escalation unfolds in discernible phases rather than sudden explosions[44,45]. Classroom-based research similarly shows that subtle shifts in posture, tone, and engagement often precede overt disruption[39]. These patterns appear across age groups and professional contexts.

The Phases of Escalation

Trigger Phase
This is the moment when something sparks emotional discomfort. It may be obvious, such as a harsh tone, a public correction, or a perceived insult. It may also be subtle: a microaggression, an unmet expectation, a sensory overload, or a reminder of past harm. For individuals with trauma histories, triggers can be relational, symbolic, or physiological, such as feeling ignored, disrespected, trapped, or unsafe.

Physiologically, the amygdala activates, and the nervous system shifts toward survival mode. Attention narrows. Cognitive flexibility decreases. The body prepares to defend[41,42].

Escalation Phase
As stress builds, behavior becomes more reactive. Signs include raised voices, rapid speech, clenched muscles, sarcasm, rigid posture, or emotional withdrawal. Logical reasoning becomes less accessible. At this stage, relational cues matter more than facts. A perceived lack of respect or control can intensify the response.

Qualitative studies of teacher responses to disruptive behavior demonstrate that this phase often begins with subtle behavioral changes that are misread as attitude or noncompliance rather than distress[39]. Without early relational repair, stress continues to accumulate.

Crisis or Peak Phase
At the height of escalation, verbal or physical outbursts may occur. This can include yelling, refusal, walking out, or emotional flooding. At this point, reasoning often fails. De-escalation focuses on safety, not resolution. Research on agitation response teams emphasizes that containment, reduced stimulation, and calm presence are central goals at this stage[45,44].

De-escalation or Recovery Phase
Once the peak passes, the nervous system begins to recalibrate. Breathing slows. Cognitive processing gradually returns. Individuals may experience shame, confusion, or regret. Support and patience—rather than interrogation—help restore dignity and invite repair[46,43].

Resolution or Reflective Phase
When safety is re-established, this phase allows for problem-

solving, reconnection, and mutual understanding. With the right support, this moment can strengthen rather than weaken relationships. Follow-up conversations, boundary clarification, and restorative practices may occur here.

Understanding these phases allows professionals to distinguish between moments that call for interpretation and moments that call for containment.

Common Triggers in High-Stress Work Environments

Across sectors, common escalation triggers include:

- perceived disrespect or dismissal
- feeling unheard or overcontrolled
- sudden policy enforcement without explanation
- physical discomfort (heat, noise, fatigue)
- lack of autonomy or predictability
- trauma reminders such as tone of voice, uniforms, or isolation

For employees, organizational stressors such as unclear communication, perceived unfairness, and chronic workload strain can also activate the escalation cycle[47,46].

Research in trauma-sensitive schools and behavioral health systems demonstrates that unpredictable environments and inconsistent boundaries increase the frequency of behavioral incidents regardless of individual temperament[48,49]. These findings highlight that escalation is shaped not only by individuals but by the conditions in which they operate.

The Role of the Nervous System

Escalation does not originate in character; it originates in the body. When conflict arises, the nervous system activates survival responses shaped by biology and experience. These responses are not chosen. They are automatic.

The autonomic nervous system regulates heart rate, breathing, and arousal. During a perceived threat, the sympathetic nervous system mobilizes the fight-or-flight response. In trauma, the parasympathetic system may also elicit a freeze or fawn response. These reactions arise in the brainstem and limbic system, often bypassing conscious thought to prioritize survival[8,50,41].

Under threat, the prefrontal cortex—the region responsible for judgment, impulse control, and planning—becomes less accessible[51]. This explains why people in escalation may struggle to process language, consider alternatives, or reflect on consequences.

Professionals who understand these mechanisms respond with less personalization and greater emotional steadiness[40]. Calm and fear are both contagious.

Fight, Flight, Freeze, and Fawn: Nervous System Responses

These survival responses manifest behaviorally:

Fight: aggression, argument, control-seeking, rigid posture
Flight: avoidance, leaving, disengagement
Freeze: shutdown, silence, immobility
Fawn: appeasement, over-agreement, masking needs[20]

In professional contexts, these may appear as absenteeism, excessive compliance, confrontational tone, or emotional withdrawal. Understanding them depersonalizes conflict and supports accurate interpretation.

The Autonomic Nervous System and Stress Response

The autonomic nervous system has two primary branches relevant to conflict response. The sympathetic nervous system activates during perceived threat, preparing the body to fight or flee by increasing heart rate and releasing stress hormones such as cortisol and adrenaline. The parasympathetic nervous system restores calm, but under trauma, it may also trigger freeze or fawn responses; shutdown or appeasement behaviors that aim to preserve safety.

These responses originate in subcortical brain regions and bypass logical thought. They are not deliberate choices but instinctive adaptations[8,50].

Understanding the Four Fs

Fight
Fight responses appear as aggression, argument, control-seeking, or refusal. This is not necessarily violence. It may include sharp tone, rigid posture, or confrontational language. For professionals, it can also manifest as authoritative posturing or overcorrection. The goal is to restore safety through dominance.

Flight
Flight appears as avoidance, leaving the room, physical distancing, or restlessness. In professional settings, it may look like absenteeism, quick exits from meetings, or refusal to engage. What appears as disengagement may be an attempt to escape perceived danger.

Freeze
Freeze involves shutdown—difficulty speaking, thinking, or

moving. This may be misinterpreted as defiance or disinterest but is a protective dissociation. In schools and correctional settings, freeze is often labeled "noncompliance" when it reflects neurological overwhelm.

Fawn

Fawn responses involve appeasement and excessive compliance. People may over-apologize, agree to things they do not support, or mask their feelings to avoid conflict. Rooted in relational trauma, fawning often leads to burnout and moral injury over time[20].

Workplace Implications of the Four Fs

In schools, hospitals, government agencies, and community organizations, these responses shape daily interactions:

Individuals in freeze may not be able to answer questions even when they hear them.

A fawning employee may avoid conflict by saying yes too often, suppressing concerns.

Staff in fight mode may not be hostile personalities, but people trying to regain control under threat.

Flight responses may explain chronic avoidance rather than apathy.

When these patterns are understood, conflict can be de-personalized and redirected with empathy[40,44].

Trauma's Lasting Impact on Stress Response

For those with adverse childhood experiences or cumulative trauma, the nervous system becomes hypervigilant and more easily triggered. This increases the likelihood of interpreting neutral situations as dangerous and responding with disproportionate intensity[41,51].

This does not mean individuals are overly sensitive. It means their internal alarm system has been recalibrated for survival.

Trauma's Role in Escalation and Misinterpretation

In moments of stress, people do not always behave as expected. A child refuses to speak. An employee walks out of a meeting. A client avoids eye contact or laughs inappropriately. These behaviors are often misunderstood. Beneath them, however, frequently lies trauma rather than defiance.

Trauma alters how the brain interprets the present through the lens of the past. The amygdala becomes hypervigilant while the prefrontal cortex becomes less accessible under threat[42]. This creates what is often described as a trauma filter—a tendency to interpret ambiguous cues as danger.

A raised voice may sound threatening.
A closed door may recall entrapment.
A directive may feel like control rather than guidance.

In these moments, the trauma-affected brain is not choosing to resist. It is trying to survive.

Misreading Behavior: From Misbehavior to Survival Strategy

Many trauma-informed educators and clinicians now use the phrase "behavior is communication." What appears as defiance may be a freeze response. What looks like rudeness may be an attempt at self-protection. Common misinterpretations include:

- avoidance labeled as noncompliance

- hypervigilance mistaken for attitude
- silence judged as disrespect
- over-agreeableness seen as weakness rather than fawning

When professionals misread these signals, they may escalate the situation by asserting authority, issuing discipline, or withdrawing support.

Escalation Cycles Fueled by Misinterpretation

Misinterpretation produces predictable escalation loops:

Trigger → survival response → professional misreading → corrective authority → increased threat perception → crisis or rupture.

This pattern is especially common in schools, healthcare settings, correctional facilities, and public service environments where structure and expectations collide with dysregulated nervous systems[43,44].

Trauma-Responsive Interpretation

Rather than asking, "What is wrong with them?" trauma-informed professionals ask, "What happened to them?"

This reframing leads to different responses:

- offering choices instead of commands
- normalizing regulation rather than demanding compliance
- recognizing protective behavior rather than personalizing it

This does not excuse harmful actions. It prevents unnecessary escalation rooted in misunderstanding.

Professional Self-Awareness

Trauma shapes professionals as well. Unresolved stress histories can lead to overreaction, shutdown, or misinterpretation. A trauma-informed stance, therefore, includes self-regulation and reflection.

When escalation is understood as a nervous system event rather than a character flaw, professionals respond with intention rather than impulse.

Case Scenario: "Why Did She Snap?"

Setting: A mid-size county human services department

Maria, a frontline case manager, finishes a stressful morning filled with back-to-back intakes, two no-shows, and a tense call from a housing agency. Exhausted, she meets Kara, a young woman referred from a domestic violence shelter.

Kara avoids eye contact, speaks softly, and answers most questions with "I don't know." When asked to sign a release form, she hesitates. Maria explains the policy again. Kara still does not comply. Maria's tone tightens: "You have to sign it, or we can't move forward."

Kara's eyes fill with tears. She stands, mutters "Forget it," and leaves.

Feeling disrespected, Maria vents to her supervisor, Denise. Denise reframes the incident:

- Kara's silence reflects freeze, not rudeness.
- Hesitation may stem from control trauma.
- Maria's firmness echoed threat rather than safety.

- The rupture emerged from perceived danger, not defiance.

Through reflection, Maria adjusts her pacing and language. She avoids ultimatums, offers choices, and checks in with, "Would it help to take a moment?" Over time, she sees fewer walkouts and more cooperation.

The escalation did not arise from aggression. It arose from misinterpretation.

While the case of Maria and Kara highlights how trauma and misinterpretation operate within a single interaction, escalation rarely occurs in isolation from its surroundings. Individual nervous system responses unfold within physical, organizational, and cultural contexts that can either stabilize or intensify distress. To fully understand escalation, professionals must examine not only what happens between people but also what happens around them.

Environmental and Organizational Factors That Fuel Conflict

Escalation is often framed as an interpersonal problem rooted in personality, attitude, or poor communication. This framing is incomplete. As with individual nervous system responses, organizational environments exert powerful influence over whether stress stabilizes or intensifies. Physical space, policies, leadership practices, workload demands, and culture all interact with individual thresholds for regulation. When these conditions are ignored, professionals are left managing symptoms rather than causes.

Environmental Design and Sensory Triggers

The physical environment directly affects emotional regulation. Crowded rooms, excessive noise, harsh lighting, lack of privacy, and unpredictable movement all elevate baseline arousal. For individuals with trauma histories or sensory sensitivities, these conditions can overwhelm regulatory capacity long before any interpersonal conflict occurs.

Common environmental contributors include:

- overcrowded or confined spaces with little personal room
- noise pollution such as loud HVAC systems, alarms, intercoms, or constant conversation
- inconsistent or harsh lighting
- chaotic or poorly organized layouts
- emotionally charged interactions occurring in public or high-traffic areas

Research in educational and clinical settings demonstrates that calmer, more predictable environments reduce both behavioral incidents and stress-related symptoms, particularly for individuals with PTSD, ADHD, autism, or anxiety[48,49]. These findings reinforce that escalation is not simply about behavior in the moment but about cumulative sensory and cognitive load.

When professionals are required to manage conflict in environments that are already dysregulating, their margin for error narrows. Small missteps are more likely to escalate into ruptures.

Workload, Role Clarity, and Burnout

Organizational stress acts as a background amplifier for escalation. Understaffing, blurred roles, and unsustainable workloads create pressure-cooker conditions in which even minor disagreements can trigger disproportionate reactions.

High demands combined with low control are strongly associated with irritability, withdrawal, and aggression across sectors. When professionals are unclear about their authority, responsibilities, or decision-making latitude, conflict becomes more personal and less predictable. Frustration is easily displaced onto colleagues, clients, or students.

In caregiving and public service professions, compassion fatigue and secondary traumatic stress further lower frustration tolerance. Research shows that repeated exposure to others' trauma without adequate support increases emotional reactivity and decreases cognitive flexibility, making escalation more likely on both sides of an interaction[52,47].

Policy and Procedural Rigidness

Even well-intentioned policies can fuel conflict when applied without flexibility or trauma awareness. Zero-tolerance discipline, rigid documentation requirements, and inflexible attendance rules often ignore context and escalate situations that might otherwise be resolved relationally.

Examples include:

- policies enforced abruptly without explanation
- rules that remove discretion from frontline staff
- procedures that punish individuals managing complex life stressors
- unclear grievance or feedback channels that leave concerns unaddressed

Systems that prioritize compliance over dignity tend to push people into defensive postures. Behavioral crisis response literature emphasizes that rigid enforcement during moments of distress increases the likelihood of escalation and rupture rather than resolution[43].

Leadership and Organizational Culture

The tone of conflict within an organization often reflects the leadership's tone. Authoritarian styles may suppress overt disagreement but increase fear-based compliance, silence, and resentment. Inconsistent rule enforcement or perceived favoritism undermines trust and fuels passive conflict.

Conversely, organizations characterized by psychological safety—where concerns can be raised without retaliation—experience fewer escalations and faster repair when conflict occurs[16]. In these environments, tension is more likely to surface early, when it can still be addressed constructively.

Leadership practices that normalize emotional suppression or discourage feedback inadvertently teach employees that safety lies in silence. Over time, unresolved issues accumulate and erupt under stress.

Mismatches Between Mission and Reality

Many public-facing professions are mission-driven. Education, healthcare, mental health, and community services attract individuals motivated by values of care, equity, and service. When organizational realities fail to support those values due to chronic understaffing, inadequate resources, or blame-shifting, moral distress emerges.

This dissonance produces:

- cynicism and emotional detachment
- mistrust of leadership
- conflict rooted in systemic betrayal rather than individual behavior

Escalation in these contexts often reflects grief, exhaustion, and loss of meaning rather than interpersonal animosity. Recognizing this dynamic allows professionals to interpret conflict more accurately and respond with greater restraint.

Cultural and Communication Mismatches

Just as physical and organizational environments shape escalation, so too do cultural frameworks for meaning-making. Communication does not occur in a vacuum; it is filtered through norms about authority, emotion, and respect. Conflict does not require malice. It often arises from misunderstanding, particularly in multicultural environments where norms for communication, authority, and emotional expression vary widely. Without cultural humility, professionals may misinterpret behavior, unintentionally escalate tensions, and reinforce systems of exclusion.

Communication Is Culturally Shaped

Communication involves more than words. Eye contact, silence, tone, pacing, physical proximity, and gestures all carry culturally specific meaning.

For example:

- sustained eye contact may signal respect in some cultures and aggression in others
- silence may indicate thoughtfulness, deference, or discomfort rather than avoidance

- volume and expressiveness may be read as passion or hostility, depending on the observer

When professionals interpret behavior solely through their own cultural lens, they risk labeling others as evasive, disrespectful, or confrontational when those individuals are simply communicating differently.

The Role of Bias and Microaggressions

Unexamined assumptions and microaggressions intensify escalation risk, particularly when combined with power differentials. Comments such as "calm down," "you're being sensitive," or "that's just policy" may invalidate lived experience, especially for individuals navigating racial, linguistic, or disability-related marginalization[22].

Trauma and culture intersect. A culturally insensitive interaction can feel retraumatizing even when harm was not intended. This compounds misinterpretation and accelerates escalation.

Cultural Humility as a De-escalation Lens

Cultural humility emphasizes curiosity, self-reflection, and accountability rather than mastery. Embedded into de-escalation, it reduces projection and creates space for trust.

Practices that support cultural humility include:

- asking rather than assuming meaning
- acknowledging power dynamics
- naming and repairing missteps
- inviting clarification instead of demanding compliance

Research across healthcare and education shows that culturally responsive communication improves engagement, safety, and satisfaction while reducing conflict-related incidents[53,26].

It is not necessary to know every culture. It is essential to remain open, reflective, and willing to learn.

When Silence Escalates: Passive Conflict and Withdrawal

Like fight-or-flight, silence and withdrawal represent nervous system strategies for preserving safety when expression feels risky. Silence is often mistaken for peace. In reality, it can be a sign of rupture. In trauma-exposed or high-pressure environments, silence may function as a survival strategy; a way to avoid further harm when speaking up feels unsafe.

Withdrawal as a Nervous System Response

Withdrawal frequently accompanies freeze or fawn responses and may present as:

- minimal verbal engagement
- avoidance of eye contact
- emotional flatness
- "going through the motions"

These behaviors are protective rather than oppositional. When misinterpreted as apathy or defiance, they often provoke corrective responses that escalate rather than resolve tension.

The Illusion of Compliance

In professional settings, silence can masquerade as cooperation. Individuals may comply outwardly while disengaging internally due to fear, burnout, or moral injury. Over time, this creates environments of surface agreement and hidden resentment.

Organizational research on silence shows that when employees believe speaking up will lead to punishment or futility, trust erodes and conflict becomes entrenched[54,47].

Cultural and Structural Contributors to Silence

Silence is shaped by culture, hierarchy, and past experience. In some contexts, open disagreement violates norms of respect. In others, prior retaliation teaches that safety lies in invisibility.

Organizations that prioritize speed, productivity, or forced positivity unintentionally suppress difficult conversations. Silence then becomes adaptive, even when costly.

Re-engaging Through Invitation

Trauma-informed de-escalation does not demand disclosure. It creates conditions for re-engagement through invitation rather than force.

Supportive approaches include:

- naming observations without judgment
- offering multiple avenues for communication
- allowing time and choice
- explicitly protecting against retaliation

When silence is treated as information rather than defiance, space opens for genuine resolution.

Key Takeaways

Escalation is not merely an interpersonal failure; it is a patterned response shaped by neurobiology, trauma, environment, culture, and systems. Physical spaces, organizational practices, and leadership behaviors can either stabilize distress or amplify threat. Cultural mismatches and silence often reflect protective strategies rather than defiance.

Understanding escalation through this broader lens allows professionals to interpret behavior more accurately and respond with restraint, dignity, and purpose.

Chapter 6

Core De-Escalation Techniques

Practical strategies to defuse tension in the moment

Not all conflicts can be prevented. Even in trauma-informed, relationship-centered, and well-organized environments, tension will rise. Someone will say the wrong thing. A need will go unmet. A history we did not know about will be touched. In schools, this may look like a student whose frustration turns into disruption, a parent who arrives already activated by prior experiences of being dismissed, or a colleague whose nervous system is carrying months of overload. In healthcare, it may be a patient whose fear presents as anger, or a family member who cannot tolerate uncertainty. In public-facing work, it may be a customer who escalates when they perceive disrespect or loss of control. These moments are not evidence that prevention failed. They are evidence that humans live inside nervous systems, and nervous systems react when safety feels uncertain.

Escalation, however, is not inevitable. It is a process, and processes can be interrupted[8]. De-escalation is the set of in-the-moment skills that reduce threat, restore dignity, and create enough regulatory space for thinking to return. It is not persuasion. It is not compliance work. It is a relational and neurological intervention aimed at protecting people and preserving trust while the situation is still fluid.

This chapter focuses on the in-the-moment skills needed to defuse a tense or spiraling situation before it leads to harm—emotional, physical, or relational. These are not one-size-fits-all scripts. They are flexible tools grounded in neuroscience, communication theory, and applied learning from high-stakes fields like education, healthcare, crisis services, and public safety[7,55,56]. Across these fields, research consistently shows that structured de-escalation training improves perceived safety, reduces coercive practices, and increases staff confidence when facing aggression, even though outcomes vary by setting and implementation quality[57,58]. In schools, rapid evidence reviews emphasize that staff benefit most when training is concrete, skill-based, and aligned across the building so that students experience predictable safety cues rather than inconsistent adult reactions. Research shows that skill-based de-escalation training that includes structured simulation and practice increases staff confidence and competence in managing conflict, supporting the value of concrete, predictable safety-oriented approaches in training[59].

Across professions, the same pattern repeats. When a nervous system perceives a threat, the brain shifts toward survival. Attention narrows. Language becomes rigid or impulsive. Tone sharpens. The body prepares to fight, flee, freeze, or appease. In these states, logic does not lead. Safety leads. The central question becomes whether the environment, especially the people in it, feels safe enough for regulation to return. De-escalation, then, is the deliberate practice of reducing threat signals and increasing safety cues while maintaining boundaries.

Importantly, these tools are for everyone. Teachers, paraprofessionals, principals, nurses, social workers, front-desk staff, supervisors, facilities workers, and peer leaders all contribute to the emotional climate of a space. Research in education has shown that adult stress and emotional regulation patterns directly influence classroom behavior and escalation cycles[60,47]. The same principle applies across workplaces: regulated professionals reduce risk; dysregulated systems increase it.

Even brief interactions can either intensify escalation or create a turning point. In a time when emotional distress and interpersonal volatility are rising across institutions, these skills are not optional. They are part of competent professional practice.

We begin where de-escalation always begins: with the responder's own nervous system.

Staying Grounded: Self-Regulation Under Stress

Before you de-escalate anyone else, you must first de-escalate yourself. This is not a motivational slogan. It is a neurobiological reality. Under stress, people do not respond primarily to what you mean; they respond to what you signal. If your nervous system is activated—tight jaw, quick movements, sharper tone, narrowed eyes—the person in front of you will read that as danger, even if your words are calm. The nervous system listens to the nervous system.

High-stress moments activate the brain's threat circuitry quickly. When perceived threat rises, the amygdala triggers rapid protective responses and suppresses prefrontal functions that support impulse control, perspective-taking, and flexible problem solving[61,62]. In the middle of an escalation, this shift can happen in both parties. The person escalating may lose access to language and self-control, and the professional responding may feel pulled toward command, correction, or withdrawal. De-escalation depends on the professional refusing to give in to that pull.

A useful reframe is that emotional regulation is not "self-control." Regulation is the capacity to return to safety. Suppression is the attempt to appear calm while remaining physiologically activated. Suppression often leaks through micro-signals: clipped tone, forced smiles, rigid posture, rushed pacing. Regulation, by contrast, changes the body state. It restores breathing, slows movement, and opens attention. Over time, repeated regulation strengthens the brain's capacity to recover from activation; this is a neuroplastic process shaped by what is practiced in real moments, not what is intended in calm ones[62].

Grounding starts with awareness. The first sign of escalation is often not the other person's behavior, but your internal shift. Professionals should learn to recognize their early signals: heat in the face, speed in the chest, tightening in the shoulders, an internal narrative that becomes judgmental or urgent. Being trauma-informed requires being body-informed. Your body often detects a threat faster than your language does[8].

Awareness creates a choice point. The choice point may be only a breath long, but it matters. A brief pause interrupts an impulsive reaction. It gives the nervous system a chance to settle before words are released into the interaction. Many professionals underestimate the power of this micro-intervention. A short pause can prevent a cascade that takes days or weeks to repair.

Grounding also involves orienting. In escalation, the brain time-travels. It anticipates danger and reacts as if the worst is already happening. Orientation returns the brain to the present. Pressing feet into the floor, softening the shoulders, lowering the chin slightly, and allowing a longer exhale are small actions with large effects. They send signals of safety to your own body and reduce the urge to perform authority through intensity.

Naming the internal state can further engage the prefrontal cortex[63]. Quietly acknowledging "I am feeling flooded" or "I am getting tense" is not indulgence; it is a cognitive intervention that helps shift the brain from threat reaction to reflective functioning. Professionals do not need to narrate these thoughts aloud. The benefit comes from the internal labeling itself.

Grounding in crisis is easier when practiced outside of crisis. While resilience practices belong more fully in later sections, there is a direct practice effect for de-escalation. Brief daily regulation habits, such as breathing exercises, reflective journaling, and peer consultation, can strengthen recovery capacity. In schools, reflective supervision has been shown to reduce burnout and improve consistency in adult responses[60]. In crisis and healthcare settings, peer check-ins reduce secondary traumatic stress and improve regulation during acute events[64,65]. This is not therapy. It is professional skill development[47].

A regulated professional protects others. In tense moments, people look for signals of safety, and leadership—formal or informal—becomes a primary signal source. Calm leadership interrupts escalating cycles. It reduces shame. It preserves dignity. In trauma-informed environments, regulation is not a private wellness practice; it is a frontline safety skill.

Self-regulation is the foundation of de-escalation, but it does not remain an individual process. In moments of conflict, regulation becomes relational. Human nervous systems continuously read and respond to one another, especially under stress. A grounded professional does more than manage their own reactions; they shape the emotional field of the interaction. This is where self-regulation becomes co-regulation: the process by which one person's steadiness helps another regain a sense of safety and control. Understanding this shift is essential because, in high-stress environments, the professional's presence often serves as the primary signal of whether a situation will escalate or stabilize.

From Self-Regulation to Co-Regulation

Co-regulation is the process by which one person's nervous system helps stabilize another's. In schools, this is a daily reality. Students often borrow regulation from the adults around them. In healthcare, patients and families calibrate fear and trust based on how staff move and speak. Co-regulation happens before content. It is carried through tone, pace, posture, and facial expression.

Co-regulation is not permissiveness. It does not mean agreeing with harmful behavior. It means lowering the threat enough for the person to regain sufficient self-control to access boundaries. Many professionals attempt to set limits while the other person is still flooded. This often fails because a flooded brain cannot process or integrate expectations. De-escalation works when regulation precedes instruction.

The professional's presence becomes a stabilizing force. Breathing, body language, and facial expression send signals long before words are processed. A steady posture, relaxed shoulders, and slower movements communicate containment. When professionals remain grounded, they interrupt escalation cycles not through authority, but through nervous system influence.

In group environments, co-regulation extends beyond the individual interaction. The emotional tone of a room shifts when one person becomes visibly calm. This is why leadership presence matters so deeply in high-stress settings. The leader's nervous system becomes a reference point for others. Calm leadership does not deny conflict; it organizes it.

This relational process also preserves dignity. When a person in distress feels regulated rather than overpowered, they are more likely to re-engage with reasoning and connection. De-escalation becomes an act of respect rather than control. The goal is not silence, but restoration of enough safety for dialogue to return.

Co-regulation also protects professionals. When boundaries are delivered from a regulated stance, they are less likely to become personal. The professional does not absorb the emotional storm; they contain it. This reduces the risk of burnout, secondary trauma, and emotional withdrawal over time.

In trauma-informed environments, co-regulation is not an optional skill. It is part of ethical practice. The professional's body and voice become tools of intervention. Regulation moves from being an internal discipline to a relational responsibility.

Verbal De-Escalation - What to Say and What to Avoid

When tension rises, words can either increase danger or restore safety. In moments of conflict, individuals are often not operating from logic but from emotion, fear, or shame. This means that the structure, pacing, and emotional tone of language matter as much as its content[55].

Verbal de-escalation is not about winning the exchange. It is about creating enough psychological safety for the reactive brain to stand down and for relational thinking to return.

Language that lowers threat tends to be slow, concrete, and respectful. It offers options rather than ultimatums. It communicates dignity even while communicating limits.

Statements that dismiss or invalidate escalate because they deny the speaker's emotional reality. Reassuring without minimizing is essential.

Table: 1

Language That Tends to Reduce Escalation

Say This	Avoid Saying This
"I'm here to listen."	"Calm down."
"You don't have to explain everything right now."	"You're overreacting."
"Let's pause for a moment."	"This isn't a big deal."
"Would it help to talk somewhere quieter?"	"You need to stop right now."
"I can see this is really upsetting."	"What is wrong with you?"
"What do you need right now?"	"Why did you do that?"
"We can work on the next step together."	"If you don't…, then…"

Validation is central. Validation is not agreement. It is acknowledgement that someone's feelings are understandable. It communicates: "You matter. You are not being judged." Validation lowers defensiveness and helps slow the body's stress response[7,27].

Instead of: "This is inappropriate behavior."
Try: "I can see how upsetting this feels. Let's slow down so we can work through it."

Language should remain concrete and paced. Under stress, working memory shrinks. Long explanations and abstract reasoning become difficult to process. Short sentences and one idea at a time are neurologically appropriate. Speaking more slowly than normal may feel unnatural, but it provides a rhythm the nervous system can mirror.

"Why" questions often escalate because they sound accusatory and demand insight when insight is least available. Replace them with:

- "What happened just before this?"
- "What do you need right now?"
- "What would help you feel safe again?"

Curiosity is validation's partner. Calm curiosity shifts interactions away from blame and toward understanding. It invites narrative rather than argument. In schools, curiosity disrupts punishment scripts. In healthcare, it interrupts fear-driven resistance. In public service, it restores agency.

Short sentences matter. Under stress, working memory shrinks. Complex explanations overwhelm. A single clear invitation— "Let's pause"—often works better than long reasoning.

Silence is also part of verbal skills. A well-timed pause allows the nervous system to recalibrate. Silence becomes helpful when paired with relaxed posture and attentive presence.

Consistency across staff is critical. PBIS research demonstrates that predictable adult responses reduce student escalation and increase behavioral stability[10]. Inconsistent language creates uncertainty, which increases threat. Shared phrasing supports safety not through scripting but through coherence.

Cultural humility remains essential. Communication norms vary across communities[53,22]. Direct eye contact, tone, and pacing can be interpreted differently. De-escalation requires curiosity about meaning rather than assumption about intent.

Nonverbal Communication - Tone, Proximity, and Presence

In moments of conflict, people attend more to how something is communicated than to what is communicated. Tone, posture, and proximity send rapid cues about safety, threat, and intent. For trauma-exposed individuals, these cues carry particular weight.

Nonverbal presence is not background behavior. It is an intervention.

The tone of voice often serves as the first signal. A raised or urgent tone activates threat responses. A lower, slower tone supports downregulation and communicates containment rather than alarm.

Proximity is equally powerful. Trauma-informed practice emphasizes respecting personal space. Standing too close can feel coercive or dangerous, particularly for those with histories of boundary violation. Approaching at an angle rather than head-on reduces confrontation. Maintaining a clear path to an exit reduces the sense of being trapped.

Body language should convey predictability: arms relaxed, hands visible, movements slow and intentional. Nervous gestures such as pacing, pointing, or crossed arms can unintentionally escalate conflict.

Facial expression matters. Flat affect can feel cold; exaggerated expression can feel patronizing. A regulated face—soft eyes, relaxed brow, attentive posture—serves as an emotional anchor.

Congruence is essential. When words say "You are safe" but the body says "I am nervous," people notice. Trauma survivors are especially sensitive to this mismatch. Stillness is often an advanced de-escalation skill. While anxiety drives movement, stillness communicates containment.

Table: 2

Nonverbal Signals That Influence Escalation

Support Regulation	Escalate Threat
Slow, steady tone	Sharp or urgent tone
Standing at an angle	Standing directly in front
Hands visible and relaxed	Pointing or clenched fists
Stillness and calm posture	Pacing or looming
Soft eye contact	Staring or glaring

Empathy and Calm Curiosity Without Enmeshment

At the center of most escalations is a human need that feels threatened, including respect, safety, fairness, control, or dignity. Empathy and curiosity are tools for locating that need and responding without increasing threat.

Empathy is not sentimentality. It is a neurological regulator. When a person feels seen and validated, the brain can shift from threat to cognitive functioning.

Empathy is most effective when it is immediate, sincere, and specific:

"It looks like this feels really unfair."
"This seems overwhelming right now."

Calm curiosity is empathy's partner. Curiosity invites narrative rather than argument and protects against assumption:

"Help me understand what feels most important right now."
"Is there something I'm missing?"

Empathy must not become enmeshment. Professionals can absorb emotional intensity and lose clarity about limits, leading to burnout. Calm curiosity creates engagement without over-identification. Empathy without boundaries drains professionals; boundaries without empathy escalate others.

Empathy must extend to the person who is escalating, not only to bystanders. Trauma-informed de-escalation separates understanding from excusing. The behavior may be unacceptable, but the human need beneath it remains real.

Cultural humility is essential. Communication norms vary across cultures. Microaggressions and unexamined bias can escalate interactions. De-escalation requires curiosity about meaning rather than judgment about behavior.

Table 3: Empathy vs. Enmeshment

Empathy (Regulating)	Enmeshment (Draining)
Names feelings	Absorbs emotional burden
Maintains boundaries	Loses role clarity

Invites narrative	Pressures disclosure
Preserves dignity	Creates dependence

Time, Space, and Pacing as Core Tools

One of the most overlooked de-escalation strategies is time. When emotions peak, pressure to resolve the situation immediately often increases escalation rather than reducing it. The nervous system needs time to downshift from threat response to reflective capacity. Forcing resolution too soon can harden positions and intensify emotional flooding.

Creating space is both literal and psychological. Literal space involves moving to a quieter location, reducing sensory input, or allowing physical distance between individuals. Psychological space involves slowing conversation, removing an audience, and reducing performance pressure.

In classrooms, allowing a student to step out briefly can prevent full behavioral collapse. In healthcare, stepping away from a bedside during agitation may preserve dignity. In workplaces, delaying a disciplinary conversation until emotions have settled often leads to more productive outcomes.

Time also protects professionals. Without space to reset, staff accumulate unresolved stress that compounds across the day. Research on burnout demonstrates that repeated exposure to conflict without recovery time increases emotional exhaustion and reduces empathy over time[66,67].

Time and space should not be framed as avoidance. They are containment strategies. They acknowledge that not all problems can be solved in a single moment and that safety must precede solutions.

Table 4: Time and Space as De-Escalation Tools

Strategy	Effect
Brief pause before responding	Interrupts impulsive reaction
Offering quieter location	Reduces sensory load
Standing back	Lowers perceived threat
Silence with steady posture	Signals patience
Choice about movement	Restores agency

Boundaries That Protect Dignity

De-escalation does not mean permissiveness. Boundaries remain essential. What changes is how boundaries are communicated. Trauma-informed boundaries are clear, calm, and consistent. They do not rely on threat, shame, or dominance.

Respectful redirection focuses on behavior, not character. It avoids labels and moral judgments. Instead of "You are being disrespectful," a trauma-informed response might say, "I can't allow yelling in this space, but I want to help you be heard." This preserves both safety and dignity.

Consistency is critical. PBIS research demonstrates that predictable adult responses reduce behavioral escalation and increase emotional security[68]. When boundaries shift with mood or authority, individuals experience uncertainty, which triggers threat responses.

Choice within limits is another core strategy. Offering small choices restores agency without surrendering structure. "Would you like to sit here or step outside?" preserves control while maintaining expectations. Autonomy is regulating.

Boundaries also protect staff. Without them, professionals become emotionally flooded or physically unsafe. Trauma-informed care includes staff safety as an ethical responsibility, not an afterthought[7].

Table 5: Boundary Language That De-Escalates

Respectful Boundary	Escalating Boundary
"I can't allow yelling here."	"You're out of control."
"Let's find a safer way."	"That's unacceptable."
"You can choose X or Y."	"Do this now."
"I want to help."	"You always do this."

Leadership boundaries model both care and accountability: "I care about your well-being, and I also need to hold this standard. Let's figure out next steps together."

Knowing When to Step Back and Call for Help

De-escalation is not always successful in the moment. Some situations exceed the capacity of one person to manage safely.

Knowing when to step back is not failure. It is professional judgment.

Warning signs that additional support is needed include:

- Escalating physical agitation
- Threats of harm
- Loss of verbal capacity
- Dissociation or panic

Environmental risk factors (crowds, confined spaces, weapons)

In these moments, shifting from individual response to team response preserves safety. Crisis protocols, behavioral response teams, and peer support systems exist for this reason. No professional should be expected to manage acute crisis alone[69,7].

Stepping back should be communicated clearly and calmly. Abrupt withdrawal can feel like abandonment. A trauma-informed transition might sound like, "I'm going to get someone who can help us through this safely." This maintains connection while expanding support.

Cross-sector research consistently shows that team-based crisis responses reduce injury, escalation, and emotional harm compared to isolated interventions[70,20].

Integrating De-Escalation into Daily Practice

These techniques do not function independently. They operate as a coordinated system: self-regulation, nonverbal presence, empathy, time and space, boundaries, and team support. When practiced regularly, they become embodied habits rather than cognitive strategies.

Experiential learning is essential. Role-plays, simulations, and reflective supervision strengthen de-escalation far more effectively than lectures alone[71,72,56]. Practice builds procedural memory so that under stress, the body knows what to do. Contemporary de-escalation curricula similarly emphasize simulation, interprofessional drills, and trigger-phase assessment training to strengthen real-time judgment[56,73].

Importantly, these skills also protect professionals from long-term harm. Compassion fatigue and secondary traumatic stress emerge when individuals repeatedly absorb distress without tools for regulation and support[64,66]. De-escalation is consequently not only a client-centered practice but a workforce sustainability strategy.

Key Takeaways

De-escalation is not a single technique. De-escalation is not about control. It is about restoring safety to a system that has temporarily lost it. It requires skill, awareness, and humility. It asks professionals to regulate themselves before regulating others, to communicate with dignity, and to recognize when help is needed.

Across schools, healthcare settings, and public-facing professions, the same truth emerges: behavior follows nervous systems. When professionals learn to work with the nervous system rather than against it, conflict becomes an opportunity for stabilization rather than harm.

De-escalation is not an emergency maneuver alone. It is a daily practice of presence, boundaries, and care—one interaction at a time.

Chapter 7

Navigating High-Risk Situations

Managing complex, volatile, or unpredictable scenarios

Even with strong prevention practices and effective de-escalation skills, some situations will rise into a zone of heightened risk. These moments may involve immediate danger, extreme emotional dysregulation, or unpredictable behavior that exceeds the reach of ordinary conflict-resolution tools. Navigating high-risk situations is not only about physical safety; it is also about preserving human dignity, restoring a sense of control, and preventing the response itself from becoming another source of trauma.

High-risk encounters demand swift, skilled, and trauma-informed action. They require professionals to integrate everything discussed in earlier chapters—self-regulation, co-regulation, communication, and boundaries—while also recognizing when the situation has shifted into a fundamentally different category of risk. This chapter explores how professionals assess and manage these moments when prevention has failed or when crisis emerges despite best efforts. The goal is not only containment, but also the creation of conditions that allow recovery and repair after the immediate danger has passed.

Crisis vs. Conflict: Knowing the Difference

One of the most consequential errors in high-stress environments is failing to distinguish between conflict and crisis. On the surface, both may involve raised voices, agitation, or emotional intensity. Yet they are governed by different neurological and psychological dynamics and require different response strategies. Misinterpreting one for the other can escalate rather than stabilize a volatile situation[74].

Conflict generally arises from disagreements over needs, values, expectations, or perspectives. It may be emotionally charged, but most individuals in conflict retain some access to reasoning, language, and goal-directed behavior. Conflict can often be addressed through communication, empathy, boundary-setting, and structured problem-solving[75]. Resolution typically involves negotiation, compromise, or mutual understanding.

Crisis is fundamentally different. Crisis reflects a breakdown in internal regulation. It is not simply an argument; it is a state in which the person's nervous system is overwhelmed by perceived or actual threat to safety, control, or survival. Crisis may be triggered by trauma histories, acute mental health symptoms, substance use, neurological differences, or environmental overload[7]. At this point, rational thinking is often inaccessible as the amygdala overrides the prefrontal cortex[42]. Communication may become ineffective or even harmful until some degree of regulation is restored.

For trauma-exposed individuals, this distinction becomes even more critical. What appears to be a manageable conflict can rapidly become a crisis when cues resemble earlier experiences of harm, humiliation, abandonment, or loss of control[76,41]. Professionals must therefore assess emotional state, not just surface behavior. Asking, Is this person disagreeing with me, or are they dysregulated? can change the entire response posture.

When a nervous system is in crisis, tools such as validation, time, nonverbal safety signals, and co-regulation are often far more effective than logic or confrontation[8]. Treating crisis as conflict invites power struggles and shame. Treating conflict as crisis risks unnecessary restriction and loss of agency. Effective practice depends on recognizing which state is present.

Table 1: Conflict vs. Crisis — Response Implications

Dimension	Conflict	Crisis
Primary driver	Disagreement, unmet needs, miscommunication	Nervous system overload, perceived threat
Cognitive capacity	Reasoning and dialogue still possible	Logic and verbal processing impaired
Emotional state	Frustrated, tense, defensive	Panicked, dissociated, aggressive, or shut down
Appropriate response	Communication, mediation, boundary-setting	Safety, co-regulation, stabilization
Role of professional	Facilitator of problem-solving	Regulator and protector of safety
Risk of misinterpretation	Can escalate if treated as defiance	Severe escalation if treated as conflict
Trauma-informed priority	Preserve dignity and restore dialogue	Restore regulation before any dialogue

Understanding this difference protects both the individual in distress and the professional responding. Conflict invites dialogue. Crisis demands safety.

Working with Individuals in Crisis or Dysregulation

When individuals enter crisis or severe dysregulation, logic and language are often the first capacities to disappear. Professionals must shift from persuasion to presence, from explanation to co-regulation. Trauma-informed practice reminds us that beneath disruptive behavior is often a nervous system overwhelmed by threat, memory, or emotional overload[8,42].

Dysregulation occurs when internal stress responses overwhelm a person's capacity to self-soothe, process information, or respond adaptively. It may manifest as yelling, crying, pacing, aggression, withdrawal, dissociation, or appearing "checked out." Dysregulation is especially common among individuals with trauma histories, mental health conditions, developmental differences, or chronic environmental stress[7,41].

Unlike someone engaged in strategic conflict, a dysregulated person is rarely trying to "win." Their behavior is driven by a limbic system interpreting danger, even when no visible threat is present. Recognizing this distinction shifts professional responses away from punishment and toward stabilization.

Several principles consistently support safer outcomes across settings.

Co-regulate first, then communicate.
When arousal is high, reasoning and verbal problem-solving are often ineffective. Co-regulation—calm tone, relaxed posture, predictable pacing, and steady presence—helps the individual's

nervous system begin to settle. Communication becomes possible only after some degree of regulation returns[8].

Safety over correction.
The priority in crisis is not teaching or discipline. It is threat reduction. This may involve lowering sensory input, increasing physical space, reducing audience effects, and offering small choices that restore agency: "Would you like to sit here or step outside?" These actions communicate control without coercion.

Validation without escalation.
Validation stabilizes when it acknowledges emotion without endorsing harmful behavior. Statements such as "I can see this is a lot right now" or "You're safe here—we'll figure this out together" reduce defensiveness. In contrast, language that minimizes ("Calm down") or controls ("You need to stop") often increases arousal.

Anchoring to the present.
Crisis pulls attention into threat memory and catastrophic prediction. Gentle orientation to the present—"You're here with me," "Let's take one breath together," "Feel your feet on the floor"—can interrupt emotional flooding[27]. Simple sensory grounding (holding an object, counting slowly, focusing on physical contact with the ground) can be more effective than verbal explanation.

Professionals must also recognize common missteps. Over-talking overwhelms already taxed cognitive capacity. Taking the behavior personally shifts the responder into threat mode. Power struggles escalate nervous systems on both sides. Abrupt disengagement can feel like abandonment, even when stepping back is necessary; when distance is required, it should be paired with reassurance that support is not being withdrawn emotionally.

These dynamics cut across professions. In schools, students with higher adversity exposure may be labeled "defiant" when they are dysregulated[20]. In healthcare, patients with trauma histories may react to routine procedures with agitation or withdrawal. In workplace or municipal settings, employees under chronic stress may destabilize during performance reviews or disciplinary conversations. The profession changes; the nervous system does not. Trauma-informed de-escalation is fundamentally a human response to human distress.

Field-Based Challenges: Isolated Locations and Public Settings

Crisis does not occur only in controlled environments. Many professionals—social workers, healthcare providers, educators, inspectors, utilities staff, and outreach teams—operate in the field, where unpredictability is high and support may be distant. Trauma-informed practice in these contexts requires more than empathy; it demands environmental awareness, boundary clarity, and advance safety planning.

Field-based work carries a distinct risk profile. Isolation reduces immediate access to help. Unfamiliar settings increase uncertainty, particularly when behavioral triggers are unknown. Public locations introduce bystanders, distractions, and performance pressure. Cultural mismatch and systemic distrust—especially involving authority figures—can intensify reactions during interventions[41].

Preparation is subsequently a form of de-escalation. Pre-engagement planning allows professionals to consider known risks, trauma histories, and environmental constraints. Partner or buddy protocols add physical safety and emotional regulation capacity;

team members can monitor one another's stress and share responsibility when tension rises[77].

Environmental awareness is essential. Professionals must attend to exits, barriers, proximity, bystanders, and objects that could be used as weapons. These assessments are not paranoid; they are protective. They allow for calm decision-making if escalation occurs.

Public settings add the complexity of bystander dynamics. When conflict unfolds in view of others—on a street, in a lobby, or at a school event—shame and audience effects can amplify intensity. Individuals may escalate to preserve dignity or control. Professionals may feel pressure to "perform" authority. Creating psychological privacy through posture and voice can reduce spectacle and restore containment. A simple redirection such as, "Let's step over here where it's quieter," can lower arousal for everyone involved.

When bystanders interfere, brief boundary language can protect the space: "We're handling something sensitive right now. Please give us room so we can support this person safely." This preserves dignity for the individual in crisis while maintaining professional authority.

After field-based incidents, professionals often return to vehicles or the next call without structured debrief or support. Organizations that rely on field work should intentionally provide reflective space, supervisor check-ins, and clinical consultation when needed[47]. Isolation does not end when the situation resolves unless systems actively counter it.

Field professionals work at the edge of predictable systems and volatile realities. Their safety depends not only on individual skill, but on organizational commitment to preparation, partnership, and post-incident care.

Table 2: High-Risk Situation Response Framework

Phase	Primary Goal	Key Actions	Trauma-Informed Lens
Recognition	Identify crisis vs. conflict	Observe behavior, assess regulation, scan environment	Ask: "Is this survival, not resistance?"
Stabilization	Reduce threat and arousal	Calm tone, space, grounding, validation	Preserve dignity and agency
Protection	Ensure the safety of all	Remove stimuli, call support if needed	Least restrictive intervention
Assessment	Evaluate risk patterns	Multidisciplinary input, behavior-focused review	Context over character
Planning	Prevent recurrence	Safety plans, staffing adjustments, referrals	Intervention, not punishment
Recovery	Support healing	Debriefing, documentation, emotional support	Prevent secondary trauma

Threat Assessment and Safety Planning

In environments where conflict and crisis are possible, a proactive approach to threat assessment and safety planning is essential. Whether in schools, healthcare systems, public agencies, or field-based work, early recognition of concerning behavior and coordinated response protocols can prevent escalation and reduce the likelihood of harm. Threat assessment is not about labeling individuals as dangerous; it is about identifying patterns of risk, intervening early, and mobilizing supports that protect both the person in distress and the surrounding community.

Threat assessment is a structured process for evaluating behaviors that may signal increasing risk to self or others. It focuses on actions and patterns rather than identity or diagnosis. Research demonstrates that targeted violence is often preceded by observable warning signs such as fixation on grievances, changes in behavior, boundary violations, and communication of intent[69,78]. Unlike profiling, which relies on assumptions, threat assessment emphasizes context, trajectory, and intervention.

Trauma-informed threat assessment recognizes that behaviors of concern often emerge from fear, loss, or unmet needs rather than malicious intent. This perspective does not minimize risk; it strengthens response by avoiding shame-based or punitive reactions that may intensify distress. A trauma-informed approach asks not only Is there danger? but also What support is needed to prevent this situation from becoming more dangerous?

Effective threat assessment relies on multidisciplinary collaboration. Mental health professionals, supervisors, educators, human resources, legal counsel, and field staff each bring essential perspectives. This diversity reduces blind spots and ensures that decisions are grounded in both safety and equity. Confidentiality and dignity must be preserved throughout the process, and the person of concern should be treated with fairness rather than suspicion whenever involvement is appropriate.

Common warning signs that warrant attention include verbal or written threats, fixation on a person or grievance, escalating agitation, boundary testing, withdrawal, inappropriate interest in weapons or past violent events, and sudden shifts in demeanor. No single behavior predicts violence. It is the pattern, intensity, and trajectory of behavior over time that guide professional judgment.

Safety planning translates assessment into action. A safety plan outlines concrete steps to reduce risk and increase stability. This may include modifying schedules, changing meeting locations, adding staff presence, arranging behavioral health support, or clarifying response protocols. Effective plans specify roles, communication pathways, and follow-up timelines. They are living documents, adjusted as conditions change.

A trauma-informed safety plan is collaborative when possible. Including the individual in parts of the planning process can restore agency and reduce adversarial dynamics. The goal is not surveillance but stabilization—creating conditions where harm becomes less likely and connection more possible.

Threat assessment and safety planning are not reserved for extreme cases. They are part of a prevention-focused culture that notices early warning signs and responds before crisis becomes catastrophe.

Workplace Violence: Prevention, Protocols, and Postvention

Workplace violence remains one of the most serious occupational hazards in frontline environments such as healthcare, education, social services, and community-based work. It includes behaviors ranging from verbal threats and intimidation to physical assault and weapon use[64]. Exposure to violence affects not only physical safety but also psychological well-being, morale, and retention.

Workplace violence is commonly categorized into four types: criminal intent, client or customer violence, worker-on-worker violence, and personal relationship violence that enters the workplace. In human service professions, the most prevalent form involves clients, students, or patients who are overwhelmed, distressed, or experiencing trauma[42].

Several structural factors increase risk: understaffing, long wait times, unclear procedures, poor environmental design, and high emotional labor. Chronic burnout and compassion fatigue further reduce tolerance for stress and increase vulnerability to conflict[52]. In underserved communities, systemic inequities such as racism, poverty, and lack of access to care can heighten emotional volatility and mistrust[41].

Prevention begins with policy. Trauma-informed policies define violence clearly, establish expectations for safety, and create reporting channels that protect employees from retaliation. Environmental design strategies such as controlled access points, visibility, and panic systems reduce opportunity for harm[79]. Training must be ongoing and include de-escalation skills, trauma awareness, environmental scanning, and scenario-based practice[26]. De-escalation is increasingly framed in professional training models as an assessment-driven, theory-grounded competency rather than a scripted response[56].

Response protocols provide structure when violence occurs. Teams should know how to initiate emergency responses, communicate with supervisors and security, document events, and provide immediate support. Rehearsing responses through simulations or tabletop exercises builds coordination and reduces confusion under stress[69].

Postvention—the response after a violent incident—is as critical as prevention. Trauma-informed postvention includes emotional support, debriefing, transparent communication, and monitoring for secondary trauma or withdrawal. Without support, employees who experience violence face increased risk of PTSD, depression, and burnout[42]. Healing is not automatic; it requires intentional care.

A culture that treats workplace violence as a systems issue rather than an individual failure fosters trust and resilience. When staff feel protected and heard, safety becomes collective rather than defensive.

Coordinating with Law Enforcement, Security, and Behavioral Health Teams

High-risk situations often exceed the capacity of any single professional or department. Effective coordination with law enforcement, security personnel, and behavioral health teams can prevent harm when threats escalate or when mental health crises require specialized intervention.

Coordination is most effective when relationships are established before crisis occurs. Memorandums of understanding, joint training, and shared protocols clarify roles and expectations.

Behavioral health partnerships—such as mobile crisis teams— offer alternatives to law enforcement-only responses, especially in situations driven by psychological distress[7,70].

Each partner brings distinct strengths. Law enforcement ensures safety when weapons or imminent danger are present. Security teams monitor environments and support containment. Behavioral health professionals assess emotional states and connect individuals to services. Trauma-informed coordination requires that these roles complement rather than compete with one another.

Several guiding principles support effective collaboration. Minimizing presence when possible reduces intimidation. Using the least restrictive intervention first preserves dignity. Assigning a lead communicator prevents confusion. Monitoring for retraumatization—particularly among marginalized populations— reduces unintended harm. Post-incident debriefing across all teams promotes learning and trust[26].

Model programs such as Crisis Intervention Teams and multidisciplinary threat assessment teams demonstrate that collaboration reduces arrests, prevents violence, and improves outcomes when implemented with care[69,70].

Trauma-informed crisis response is not about heroic individuals. It is about coordinated systems that share responsibility for safety and compassion.

Documentation and Legal Considerations After an Incident

How an organization documents a critical incident shapes legal protection, accountability, and healing. Documentation preserves an accurate record, supports regulatory compliance, and guides organizational learning. It is not merely administrative; it is part of ethical and trauma-informed practice.

Effective documentation is objective and factual. It records observable behaviors rather than judgments or diagnoses. Language should avoid blame and pathologizing. Including first-person accounts when appropriate allows multiple perspectives to be represented. Confidentiality must be maintained, and information shared only on a need-to-know basis.

Timeliness matters. Reports should be completed as soon as feasible after an incident, ideally within 24 hours. Essential components include who was involved, what occurred, where and when it happened, precipitating factors if known, actions taken to de-escalate, and follow-up steps.

Legal frameworks vary by sector but share core principles. Employees must be informed of their rights and the purpose of documentation. Healthcare and educational settings must comply with HIPAA and FERPA. Mandated reporting laws apply when incidents involve minors or vulnerable adults. Records must be stored securely and retained according to policy.

Some organizations supplement formal reports with reflective debrief logs. These are not legal documents but tools for emotional processing and improvement. When handled responsibly, they promote learning without increasing liability.

Trauma-informed documentation honors accuracy without humiliation. It allows systems to respond with care rather than blame and supports prevention by revealing patterns that need attention.

Conclusion

Navigating high-risk situations requires more than instinct. It requires discernment, preparation, collaboration, and systems that value safety alongside dignity. From threat assessment to coordinated response and careful documentation, trauma-informed practices transform a crisis from a moment of rupture into an opportunity for protection and learning. When professionals are supported by clear protocols and compassionate leadership, even the most volatile moments can be met with steadiness and care.

Chapter 8

Practicing De-Escalation as a Team Sport

Embedding de-escalation into team culture and systems

Conflict rarely affects just one person. When tension shows up in a workplace or service environment, it ripples outward—shaping team dynamics, influencing trust, and altering perceptions of safety and competence. Yet many organizations continue to treat de-escalation as an individual skill rather than a collective practice. This chapter challenges that assumption. Effective de-escalation is not simply what one person does in a heated moment; it is what the team prepares for, responds to, and learns from together.

When de-escalation becomes part of a team's culture, it no longer depends on the presence of a single "calm" person or the coincidence of ideal circumstances. Instead, it becomes a shared rhythm: defined norms, practiced roles, coordinated communication, and reflective learning. This collective approach reduces the likelihood of escalation, but just as importantly, it builds psychological safety and relational trust among staff.

In trauma-informed systems, prevention and response to conflict are organizational responsibilities embedded in hiring, onboarding, supervision, documentation, and post-incident support[80,81]. When teams develop a shared language, engage in regular practice, and hold one another accountable with respect, they are better equipped to protect not only themselves but also the dignity of those they serve.

This chapter explores how to make de-escalation a core part of team culture through peer coaching, real-time support, structured debriefing, and institutional learning. The goal is not perfection. It is presence, practice, and partnership.

De-escalation Norms, Roles, and Responsibilities

De-escalation works best when it is embedded into how a team operates rather than relying on individual instinct. Teams that establish shared norms and clearly defined roles are better prepared to intervene early, coordinate effectively, and maintain safety during tense moments. When expectations are vague or inconsistent, staff may hesitate, duplicate efforts, or unintentionally escalate situations through mixed messages.

Trauma-informed teams understand conflict not as personal failure but as a shared challenge requiring collective responsibility. This shift—from individual burden to team practice—is foundational to environments where safety and dignity are sustained over time.

What Are De-escalation Norms?

De-escalation norms are agreed-upon behaviors, language patterns, and procedures that guide staff responses when tension rises. They provide a predictable framework that reduces fear and confusion in moments of uncertainty.

Common norms include:

- Maintaining calm tone and posture
- Using person-first, nonjudgmental language
- Offering peers a "tap-out" option when overwhelmed
- Keeping hands visible and body stance non-threatening

Pausing interactions rather than forcing resolution during dysregulation

Norms should be co-created by teams rather than imposed from above. This process allows staff to surface cultural interpretations of behavior, address power dynamics, and ensure relevance to their specific context. Research on trauma-informed implementation emphasizes that sustained change depends on collective ownership and iterative review rather than one-time policy creation[81].

Assigning Clear Roles in a Crisis

During escalation, confusion often arises not from the behavior itself but from uncoordinated team responses. Clear role delineation reduces hesitation and prevents power struggles among staff.

Table 1: Coordinated Team Roles in De-Escalation

Role	Primary Function
Point Person	Leads verbal engagement with the distressed individual
Support Person	Observes and stands ready to assist or relieve
Environment Manager	Manages bystanders, noise, and physical space
Recorder	Notes key events for documentation
Debriefer	Initiates post-incident check-ins

These roles should rotate to prevent burnout and promote cross-training. In healthcare, education, and field-based services, rehearsal of these roles through drills or scenario practice increases staff confidence and coordination[72].

Creating a De-escalation Protocol

A trauma-informed protocol does more than list actions. It communicates purpose and reinforces dignity.

Core components include:

- Early signs of distress
- Who communicates and when others intervene
- Spatial relocation options
- Procedures for calling additional support
- Language guidelines (what to say and avoid)
- Immediate post-event actions

Protocols should be concise, accessible, and integrated into onboarding and refresher training.

Team Accountability Without Blame

Blame silences learning; shared responsibility strengthens it. Trauma-informed accountability emphasizes reflection rather than punishment. Teams grow safer when they use incidents as opportunities to examine systems rather than individuals.

Key practices include:

- Learning-focused debriefs
- Real-time peer coaching
- Naming when norms are upheld
- Addressing breakdowns respectfully

When staff trust that mistakes will be met with curiosity rather than condemnation, they remain engaged and responsive.

Conclusion

Embedding de-escalation into team culture begins with shared norms and defined roles. It is not a matter of personal temperament but of collective practice. Teams that build habits of communication, support, and reflection transform moments of tension into opportunities for safety and trust.

Practicing Scenarios and Role-Plays

De-escalation cannot be learned through theory alone. Teams must practice before crisis tests them. Scenario-based training builds muscle memory, emotional awareness, and coordination.

Experiential learning research demonstrates that skills are retained and transferred more effectively when individuals actively engage and reflect rather than passively receive information[71]. Practicing also exposes emotional triggers and highlights gaps in understanding.

What Makes a Good Scenario?

- Effective scenarios mirror real workplace challenges:
- Agitation, withdrawal, or sudden escalation
- Public and confined settings
- Power imbalances (student–adult, client–provider)
- Different escalation stages

Even subtle tensions provide valuable learning opportunities.

Building Role-Play Into Team Culture

Rather than annual trainings only, teams benefit from short, regular practice:

- 10–15 minute scenario discussions during meetings
- Rotating facilitators
- A scenario bank of anonymized real incidents
- Cross-department participation

Regular practice reduces fear of conflict and normalizes reflection.

Feedback That Builds, Not Shames

Debriefing should be structured and psychologically safe:

- Self-reflection
- Observational feedback
- Facilitator framing
- Practical takeaway

Avoid turning role-plays into performance evaluations. Growth emerges from shared learning.

Conclusion

De-escalation becomes embodied through repetition and repair. Role-plays transform readiness from abstract knowledge into practiced coordination.

Peer Support and On-the-Spot Coaching

In high-stress environments, peer support often determines whether situations escalate or stabilize. While training provides tools, trusted colleagues provide real-time regulation.

Peer support has been shown to reduce burnout and improve emotional resilience in healthcare, education, and social services[82,83].

Forms of Peer Support

- Tactical backup
- Nonverbal reassurance
- Tag-team communication
- Grounding reminders

These actions prevent emotional flooding and sustain engagement.

The Role of On-the-Spot Coaching

Real-time coaching stabilizes rather than criticizes. Quiet prompts such as "Let's pause" or "Try a softer tone" reinforce skill use without undermining authority.

Post-incident questions support reflection:

- "How are you holding up?"
- "What did you notice?"
- "Want to talk it through?"

Building a Peer Support Culture

Effective peer support requires:

- Permission
- Training
- Trust
- Time

It must be embedded in onboarding and supervision.

Power and Identity Considerations

Hierarchies and cultural dynamics shape comfort with vulnerability. Trauma-informed coaching requires sensitivity to these differences and to inclusive norms[84].

Conclusion

De-escalation thrives in relational ecosystems. When peers support one another before, during, and after difficult moments, teams develop emotional strength and institutional stability.

Conflict Debriefing: Turning Tension Into Learning

In trauma-informed, conflict-prone work environments, what happens after the conflict is just as important as what happens during it. Conflict debriefing is the deliberate process of reflecting on challenging interactions—without blame—to extract lessons, improve team dynamics, and reduce the likelihood of future escalation.

Without structured debriefing, teams risk normalizing stress, burying resentment, or misinterpreting patterns of harm. With it, they create pathways for healing, insight, and better preparation.

Why Debriefing Matters

Conflict often unfolds under conditions of heightened emotion and narrowed attention. Adrenaline rises, language becomes reactive, and judgment can cloud decision-making. Debriefing allows teams to reconnect to their values and restore perspective after the nervous system has settled.

Research from healthcare, education, and crisis-response fields indicates that post-event reflection strengthens regulation, improves coordination, and enhances psychological safety[36,85,65]. Psychological safety, in turn, supports transparency, learning, and long-term resilience.

Core Elements of a Trauma-Informed Debrief

Table 2 : Trauma-Informed Debriefing Framework

Element	Description
Timeliness	Occurs soon enough to remain meaningful but not during peak emotional activation
Safety	Conducted in a nonjudgmental, non-punitive environment
Equal Voice	All involved parties are invited to share perspectives
Systems Focus	Examines contributing structures and conditions, not just individuals
Regulation First	Begins with emotional check-in before analysis

Sample Debrief Questions

What were the early signs of tension?

What helped contain the situation?

Where did things become difficult?

What unmet needs were present—ours or theirs?

What would we try differently next time?

When leaders participate with humility, they model learning over judgment and reinforce that growth emerges from reflection rather than blame.

Building Institutional Memory

Without reflection, conflict repeats itself. When debriefs are documented in a trauma-sensitive manner, they become part of organizational learning. Patterns can be identified, training gaps addressed, and systemic stressors modified.

Debrief notes do not need to be exhaustive. Brief summaries capturing what was learned and what will change can shape future practice and reinforce accountability.

Multidisciplinary Debriefing

In teams that include educators, clinicians, administrators, and security staff, multiple perspectives illuminate different dimensions of the same event. One person may interpret behavior as defiance, another as fear, another as a system breakdown. Debriefing connects these insights and prevents siloed responses[41].

When Debriefs Go Wrong

Poorly facilitated debriefs can retraumatize staff or reinforce fear. Common pitfalls include:

- Framing the process as evaluation rather than learning
- Focusing only on errors
- Ignoring power dynamics
- Asking accusatory "why" questions instead of reflective "what happened" questions

Debriefing must remain grounded in empathy and curiosity.

Conclusion

Tension becomes transformative only when examined. Debriefing is the bridge between experience and evolution.

Creating a Shared Language for Safety

When stress increases, communication often deteriorates. A shared language for safety provides teams with consistent vocabulary to describe what is happening, what is needed, and how to respond. It reduces ambiguity, aligns expectations, and strengthens cohesion.

Trauma-informed language avoids stigmatizing or punitive labels and instead emphasizes dignity and understanding[86]. The words chosen shape both perception and action.

Why Shared Language Matters

Language influences whether a person is seen as "noncompliant" or "distressed," as a threat or as someone in need of regulation. Shared language creates predictability and coordination, especially during emergencies.

Building a Common Vocabulary

Teams should examine:

- Whether terms are consistent across departments
- Whether language is respectful and trauma-informed
- Whether staff and clients interpret phrases similarly
- Whether coded language can discreetly signal distress

Table 3: Examples of Shared Language for Safety

Phrase	Purpose
"Soft assist needed"	Signals need for peer support
"Escalation in progress"	Alerts team without blame
"Regroup and re-enter"	Indicates pause for regulation
"Holding space"	Communicates supportive presence

Co-Creating Language

Shared language should be developed collaboratively with frontline staff. Invite discussion about which words feel supportive and which feel shaming. Incorporate this language into documentation, scripts, signage, and training.

Embedding Language Into Practice

- Include in onboarding
- Reinforce in supervision
- Display in cue cards or posters
- Model consistently from leadership

Language must evolve with teams and communities.

When Language Breaks Down

Under stress, judgmental language can reappear. Teams should address this reflectively rather than punitively through supervision and peer dialogue.

Conclusion

Shared language aligns action with values. It keeps the focus on the human being rather than the behavior.

Institutionalizing Respect, Reflection, and Recovery

Sustainable de-escalation requires more than skill training. It requires embedding values into the organization's daily operations so that respect, reflection, and recovery are routine rather than exceptional.

Respect as an Operational Principle

Respect manifests in:

- Inclusive policies
- Transparent communication
- Recognition of emotional labor
- Clear conduct expectations

Staff who feel respected demonstrate greater engagement and stability[80].

Reflection as a Learning Loop

Reflection should be routine through:

- Team huddles
- Peer debriefs
- Supervision
- Feedback systems

Reflection identifies patterns and addresses root causes rather than assigning blame[87].

Recovery for Individuals and Systems

Recovery applies to both staff and institutions. Exposure to repeated conflict increases risk for burnout and secondary traumatic stress[67,66].

Recovery practices include:

- Emotional processing
- Physical rest
- Protocol revision
- Closure rituals

Table 4: Embedding Team Culture Practices

Element	How to Institutionalize
Respect	Onboarding, leadership modeling, feedback systems
Reflection	Supervision, debriefs, meeting agendas
Recovery	Post-incident care, EAP access, flexible scheduling

Leadership behavior determines whether culture shifts from policy to practice.

Conclusion

Organizations that institutionalize respect, reflection, and recovery create environments where de-escalation is not episodic but systemic. These practices form the emotional and structural scaffolding that supports trauma-informed work at every level.

SECTION 3: RESILIENCE

Chapter 9

Resilience – Sustaining Well-Being in High-Stress Work

Personal and organizational strategies that build long-term capacity, mental health, and team strength

High-stress professions demand more than technical skill—they require emotional stamina, psychological flexibility, and a strong sense of purpose. Over time, even the most passionate professionals can find themselves depleted. Without systems that support recovery and resilience, stress does not merely wear down individuals—it weakens the safety and strength of entire organizations.

That is why resilience must be treated not as a personality trait, but as a critical workforce strategy.

This chapter focuses on the habits, relationships, and structural conditions that help professionals withstand the emotional toll of trauma exposure, burnout, and chronic pressure. Drawing from research on secondary traumatic stress, compassion fatigue, and occupational well-being, it explores how resilience can be intentionally cultivated through individual practices and team culture[88,39].

Importantly, resilience is not simply about personal grit. It is about prevention and sustainability. It includes supportive supervision, manageable workloads, access to reflection and rest, culturally grounded healing practices, and community care[80,89]. It also involves confronting moral injury and systemic injustice—factors that often go unaddressed in traditional stress management models[90,86].

Through research, case studies, and insights from professionals in the trenches, this chapter offers a roadmap for building capacity—not just to keep going, but to recover and grow in meaningful ways. When we protect those who do the work, we protect the integrity of the work itself.

What Resilience Really Means in the Workplace

Resilience is often misunderstood as toughness, detachment, or simply "powering through." In high-stress professions, that misunderstanding can be dangerous. True resilience is not about denying stress or pretending to be unaffected—it is about recognizing the impact, accessing support, recovering well, and returning with purpose and clarity. Resilience is the ability to bend without breaking, to acknowledge struggle without losing hope, and to adapt without abandoning one's values.

In trauma-exposed work, resilience is a necessary survival skill—but it is also a foundation for ethical, sustainable practice.

Resilience Is a Skillset, Not Just a Trait

While some people may have natural temperaments or life experiences that strengthen their coping abilities, resilience is not fixed. It is a set of skills and behaviors that can be taught, practiced, and reinforced[91]. These include emotional regulation, cognitive reframing, social connection, help-seeking behaviors, and meaning-making. These skills are strengthened through reflection, peer support, supervision, and workplace culture[20,72].

Research consistently shows that resilient professionals are not immune to stress or trauma, but they are more likely to recover well and retain their sense of purpose[26,88].

Personal vs. Organizational Resilience

Much of the conversation around resilience focuses on the individual—but that is only half the equation. A resilient workplace is one that does not depend solely on individuals to "be strong." It creates conditions that support people in being strong together[80,88].

This includes:

Reasonable workloads and boundaries around overtime

Supportive supervision and peer connection

Opportunities for feedback, learning, and rest

Embedded policies that support mental health and psychological safety

When leaders model vulnerability, promote shared accountability, and allow space for emotional processing, they create an environment where resilience can thrive[89].

Resilience Is Not Endurance Alone

One of the most harmful myths in high-stress professions is the glorification of self-sacrifice. Overextension is too often praised as dedication. Yet unchecked self-neglect is a significant risk factor for burnout, turnover, and secondary trauma[83,66,42].

Resilience involves pacing. It requires knowing when to press forward and when to pause. It encourages people to acknowledge when they are at their limit and to access resources before reaching a breaking point.

The Role of Meaning and Purpose

In high-stress environments, meaning is a powerful buffer against burnout. Professionals who remain connected to purpose report greater resilience even under sustained emotional strain[92,88]. This does not require romanticizing suffering; it requires reaffirming that both the work and the worker matter.

Cultivating resilience means making space for storytelling, reflection, recognition, and connection to the "why" of the work. It also means redefining success in ways that honor effort, growth, and impact—not only outcomes.

Conclusion: Resilience as a Collective Commitment
In trauma-exposed environments, resilience is not solely a personal journey—it is a workplace commitment. When organizations normalize asking for help, taking breaks, and talking openly about stress, they create safer environments for everyone. Resilience does not mean never falling; it means having the tools, relationships, and space to get back up.

Compassion Fatigue, Burnout, and Moral Injury

Helping professionals often enter their fields with a deep sense of purpose. Over time, repeated exposure to trauma, systemic barriers, and emotionally taxing environments can erode that sense of calling. Three major experiences frequently emerge: compassion fatigue, burnout, and moral injury. Though related, each represents a distinct form of occupational distress requiring different responses.

Compassion Fatigue: The Cost of Caring

Compassion fatigue is the emotional and physical exhaustion that develops from prolonged exposure to others' trauma and suffering[83]. Unlike burnout, which is rooted in systemic workplace demands, compassion fatigue is tied specifically to empathic engagement.

It may present as emotional numbing, irritability, sleep disturbance, and reduced empathy. Educators and clinicians working with trauma-impacted populations experience elevated rates of secondary traumatic stress and compassion fatigue that affect professional functioning and relationships[39].

Burnout: When the System Wears You Down

Burnout is driven primarily by workload, time pressure, insufficient support, and lack of recognition[42]. It manifests as exhaustion, cynicism, reduced efficacy, and emotional detachment. Burnout has been documented extensively across education and healthcare, where it correlates with lower quality of care and higher turnover[82,88].

Moral Injury: The Pain of Ethical Betrayal

Moral injury refers to the suffering that arises when professionals are forced to act in ways that violate their ethical values or are prevented from acting according to them[90]. It often produces shame, guilt, and loss of professional identity. Trauma-informed healthcare research suggests that many providers experience not simply exhaustion but ethical distress when systems prioritize efficiency over care[86].

Table 1: Overlap and Differentiation

Experience	Primary Driver	Key Symptoms
Compassion fatigue	Empathic exposure to trauma	Emotional numbing, detachment
Burnout	Systemic work stress	Exhaustion, cynicism
Moral injury	Ethical conflict	Shame, disillusionment

Addressing these conditions requires organizational accountability, not just individual coping[88,89].

Conclusion

These are normal human responses to abnormal conditions. Naming compassion fatigue, burnout, and moral injury allows individuals and systems to pursue healing rather than blame.

Risk Factors for Helping Professionals and First Responders

Professionals who serve on the frontlines of human vulnerability—teachers, social workers, clinicians, law enforcement officers, emergency responders—carry a unique burden. Their roles demand emotional resilience, rapid decision-making, and ethical clarity, often in the face of crisis or tragedy. While these professions appear distinct, the risk factors they face are strikingly similar.

This subchapter examines the structural, interpersonal, and psychological conditions that increase vulnerability to burnout, secondary traumatic stress (STS), and compassion fatigue across caregiving professions.

Chronic Exposure to Human Suffering

Helping professionals are frequently exposed to trauma—not necessarily their own, but the trauma of others. This secondary exposure is a well-documented risk factor for STS, particularly in professions such as teaching and social work, where workers often lack formal training or institutional support to process what they witness[83,93].

Teachers working in high-adversity classrooms regularly encounter students whose behavior reflects family violence, homelessness, or chronic stress. Research shows that student dysregulation and trauma-related behavior patterns place sustained emotional strain on educators, especially when behavioral support systems such as PBIS or trauma-informed frameworks are inconsistently implemented[72,20]. Over time, repeated exposure to students' emotional crises without adequate processing can mirror the effects of direct trauma exposure.

First responders and healthcare professionals face even more direct sensory exposure to crisis and death. Without recovery time, cumulative exposure contributes to intrusive thoughts, hypervigilance, emotional numbing, and physiological stress responses that persist beyond the workplace[94].

Role Overload and Administrative Pressure

Across professions, workload and conflicting role expectations consistently emerge as major predictors of burnout. Teachers must balance instructional demands, classroom management, documentation, and family engagement under high-stakes accountability systems. Social workers and healthcare providers juggle productivity requirements alongside emotionally complex human needs. Emergency personnel manage unpredictable schedules and prolonged shifts.

Maslach and Leiter[42] describe burnout as a mismatch between job demands and available resources. When professionals have little control over pace, decision-making, or workload, emotional exhaustion intensifies. Research on educator wellbeing confirms that administrative burden and lack of planning time amplify stress more than student behavior alone[88,95].

Emotional Competence and Regulation Capacity

Savina's[20] conceptual model of teacher emotional competence highlights emotion regulation as a critical protective factor. Professionals with limited capacity to recognize and modulate their emotional responses are more vulnerable to escalation, disengagement, and secondary trauma. Emotional competence influences not only personal wellbeing but also classroom climate and client interactions.

Low emotional awareness increases the likelihood that professionals will interpret stress as personal failure rather than a nervous system response. Over time, this internalization contributes to shame-based burnout and moral distress.

Lack of Supportive Supervision

Supportive supervision is among the strongest buffers against professional distress. Yet many helping professionals report feeling blamed, ignored, or evaluated rather than emotionally supported. Loomis et al.[39] found that social work students in trauma-heavy placements experienced greater vulnerability when supervision focused on compliance instead of emotional processing.

Without psychologically safe spaces for reflection, distress becomes internalized. This dynamic fuels avoidance, detachment, and professional isolation—hallmarks of compassion fatigue and moral injury.

Cumulative and Historical Trauma

Professionals from marginalized communities often carry the burden of historical and ongoing oppression in addition to workplace trauma. A Black educator in an under-resourced school or an Indigenous healthcare worker serving a community impacted by generational trauma may experience layered stressors that amplify emotional labor[37,41].

Intersectional identities related to race, gender, sexual orientation, disability, or immigration status increase exposure to microaggressions and systemic inequities, compounding vulnerability.

Isolation in Crisis-Driven Workplaces

High-pressure environments often discourage emotional expression. First responders, nurses, and correctional officers frequently report cultural norms of stoicism that equate vulnerability with weakness. Over time, this culture of silence becomes a risk factor in itself.

Without peer dialogue or structured debriefing, stress accumulates silently and manifests as withdrawal, cynicism, or health decline.

Table 2: Risk Factors Across Levels

Level	Risk Factor	Supporting Literature
Individual	Secondary trauma exposure	Figley[83]; Savina[20]
Relational	Lack of peer support	Patrick et al., 2024; Fallon et al., 2023
Organizational	Workload and role overload	Maslach & Leiter[42]; Berger et al.[88]
Cultural/Systemic	Identity-based stress	Sotero[37]; Shonkoff et al.[41]

Conclusion: Risk Is Not Weakness

Experiencing distress in high-stakes, trauma-exposed roles is not a sign of personal failure. It is the expected result of systems that overextend human capacity without adequate safeguards. Risk factors can be addressed—but only when organizations recognize them as legitimate threats to wellness and performance.

Naming these risks is the first step toward cultural change. The next is building systems that expect, normalize, and respond to the psychological needs of those who serve.

Protective Factors That Buffer Stress and Trauma

Helping professionals and first responders operate in emotionally demanding environments where trauma exposure, high workloads, and systemic pressures are common. Yet many individuals continue to show remarkable resilience. Protective factors—supports and conditions that buffer against psychological harm—do not eliminate stress but reduce its impact and promote recovery.

This subchapter examines individual, relational, and organizational protective factors supported by current research.

Individual-Level Protective Factors

Self-Awareness and Emotional Regulation
Professionals who can recognize emotional cues and regulate stress responses show lower levels of burnout and secondary trauma[20,93]. Emotional awareness allows individuals to distinguish between situational stress and internalized failure.

Meaning and Purpose
Connection to purpose buffers against emotional exhaustion. Madigan et al.[47] found that professionals who maintained

alignment between personal values and occupational roles demonstrated higher resilience and lower disengagement.

Mindfulness and Self-Compassion
Mindfulness-based interventions reduce emotional reactivity and improve presence during difficult encounters[72,89]. These practices foster nonjudgmental awareness of stress rather than suppression.

Relational-Level Protective Factors

Peer Support and Debriefing
Strong peer networks reduce isolation and normalize emotional processing. Doyle et al.[20] demonstrated that peer support programs increased retention and psychological well-being across healthcare settings.

Supervision and Mentorship
Supportive supervision that integrates emotional check-ins is consistently associated with lower burnout and higher professional longevity[38].

Family and Community Ties
Personal relationships outside work offer refuge and perspective, reinforcing emotional grounding and identity beyond professional roles[91].

Organizational-Level Protective Factors

Trauma-Informed Organizational Culture
Workplaces that embrace trauma-informed principles—psychological safety, transparency, and shared decision-making—report higher morale and lower turnover[80].

Structured Debriefing and Recovery Time
Built-in reflection periods following critical incidents reduce cumulative trauma and restore regulation[93].

Fairness, Voice, and Recognition
When workers feel heard and valued, emotional resilience increases even under strain[95,20].

Table 3: Evidence-Based Protective Factors

Level	Protective Strategy	Supporting Evidence
Individual	Mindfulness & emotion regulation	Cetin et al.[72]; Savina[20]
Relational	Peer support & debriefing	Doyle et al.[20]; Fallon et al.[38]
Organizational	Trauma-informed leadership	Ko et al.[80]; Leading Organizations article

Conclusion

While risk is inherent in caregiving professions, resilience can be embedded as infrastructure. Protective factors act like scaffolding: they redistribute emotional load and promote recovery. Investment in individual habits, workplace culture, and systems of care determines whether resilience becomes sustainable or symbolic.

Cultural Resilience, Collective Identity, and Historical Strength

Resilience is often framed as an individual attribute, but for many communities—particularly those that have endured historical oppression, displacement, or systemic marginalization—resilience is also collective and cultural. Cultural resilience refers to the strength drawn from shared heritage, identity, values, and traditions that enable individuals and groups to navigate adversity together. While trauma can be transmitted across generations, so too can resilience—through language, ritual, memory, and community care.

This broader understanding challenges narrow psychological models of resilience that emphasize personal coping while overlooking social and historical context. In high-stress professions, especially those serving marginalized populations, resilience must be understood as both personal and communal.

Understanding Cultural Resilience

Cultural resilience is the capacity of a group to withstand and recover from adversity by drawing upon collective traditions, belief systems, and identity[96]. It includes:

- Cultural continuity: preserving and passing down language, practices, and values
- Collective memory: honoring shared histories of survival and resistance
- Cultural expression: using art, music, storytelling, and ritual to sustain meaning

These elements create coherence in the face of disruption. After disasters, violence, or displacement, cultural meaning-making often becomes the primary mechanism through which grief is processed and purpose restored.

Research on historical trauma shows that communities affected by systemic violence may experience intergenerational stress, but also intergenerational resilience when identity and cultural pride are preserved[37,97]. This dual inheritance underscores why resilience cannot be separated from history.

Historical Strength and Survival Narratives

Many communities of color, Indigenous groups, immigrants, and refugees carry histories marked by colonization, enslavement, forced migration, and structural exclusion. Yet these histories also contain powerful survival narratives. From the African American church's role in sustaining hope and resistance, to Indigenous land-based traditions that reinforce belonging and continuity, cultural memory becomes a wellspring of strength rather than only a reminder of loss.

These narratives function as what some scholars call "resistance memory"—stories that transmit courage, dignity, and meaning across generations. Such memory informs present-day identity and collective action, shaping how individuals interpret stress and injustice[96,37].

Research suggests that strong cultural identity is associated with lower rates of depression and higher levels of post-traumatic growth in communities facing chronic adversity[97]. In this way, intergenerational resilience can counterbalance intergenerational trauma.

Collective Identity in the Workplace

In high-stress professional environments such as education, healthcare, and public service, collective identity among staff can serve as a stabilizing force. Shared values, affirming language, and inclusive rituals foster belonging and solidarity—key ingredients for emotional endurance.

Workplaces that acknowledge and celebrate cultural diversity often demonstrate stronger cohesion and lower turnover. By contrast, environments that suppress or ignore cultural identity may intensify alienation and stress, particularly for staff who already experience marginalization[41].

Examples of collective identity practices include:

- Multilingual communication and signage
- Affinity groups or staff circles
- Recognition of cultural holidays and histories
- Trauma-informed approaches that consider cultural grief and healing
- Such practices move resilience beyond individual coping and into organizational culture.

Cultural Humility and Inclusive Resilience Building

Activating cultural resilience requires cultural humility—an ongoing commitment to reflection, learning, and respect for lived experience. Leaders must avoid assuming that wellness initiatives are culturally neutral. One-size-fits-all stress management programs often fail to resonate with diverse staff because they ignore spiritual, communal, or historical dimensions of healing.

Inclusive resilience-building includes:

- Inviting culturally diverse staff into program design
- Recognizing how systemic inequities affect stress differently
- Valuing community-based healing practices alongside clinical models

When organizations honor cultural identity rather than treating it as peripheral, they strengthen both morale and trust.

Conclusion

Cultural resilience reminds us that strength is often collective before it is individual. Healing and endurance arise from relationships, rituals, and shared meaning as much as from personal grit. Especially in trauma-exposed professions, resilience must expand to include the histories, voices, and cultural strengths of the communities professionals serve—and the ones in which they work.

Stories of Survival: Lessons from the Field

Resilience is not an abstract concept. It lives in classrooms, emergency rooms, and community agencies where professionals face the emotional weight of human suffering each day. These stories do not illustrate invulnerability; they reveal adaptation, boundary setting, and reconnection with purpose.

This section draws from lived experiences of educators, social workers, and first responders to show how resilience develops in practice—not through perfection, but through support, reflection, and repair.

Case 1: The Educator Who Stays

Maria, a middle school teacher in a high-needs district, described the emotional toll of watching students struggle with poverty and violence. After her first few years, she considered leaving the profession. Her turning point came when a colleague invited her to a mindfulness-based teacher support group, where she realized she was not alone.

She began practicing grounding techniques and advocating for trauma-informed practices within her school. Over time, she became a leader in staff wellness initiatives.

Key Takeaways:

- Peer support reduces burnout
- Resilience includes knowing when to seek help
- Mindfulness and community sustained her practice

Research Connection:
Maria's experience reflects findings that mindfulness-based and peer-supported interventions improve emotional regulation and reduce secondary trauma in educators[72,89,20].

Case 2: The Paramedic's Pause

Jason, a paramedic with ten years of experience, began dissociating during routine emergencies after a difficult pediatric call. Through counseling and peer debriefing, he learned to identify his emotional thresholds and seek help earlier.

His therapist's reminder—"Your nervous system wasn't meant to do this alone"—became a guiding principle.

Key Takeaways:

- Structured debriefing prevents cumulative trauma
- Supervisors who normalize help-seeking foster healing
- Naming distress restores agency

Research Connection:
Debriefing and peer support have been shown to reduce PTSD symptoms and improve psychological safety among first responders[38,94].

Case 3: The School Social Worker Who Set Boundaries

Angela, the sole mental health provider for 400 students, reached burnout after months of nonstop crisis response. With clinical supervision, she implemented time boundaries, reduced session loads, and advocated for systemic change.

She also began journaling to process vicarious trauma.

Key Takeaways:

- Boundaries are essential to sustainability
- Advocacy is part of self-care
- Reflection builds clarity and resilience

Research Connection:
Savina's[20] model of emotional competence and Fallon et al.[38] work on supervision support the role of reflection and regulation in preventing burnout.

Cross-Cutting Lessons in Professional Resilience

Across these stories, consistent themes emerge:

- Connection protects: Peer relationships buffer stress
- Boundaries buffer: Sustainable service requires limits
- Identity matters: Cultural and community ties strengthen purpose
- Reflection transforms: Meaning-making fosters growth

These patterns mirror research showing that resilience depends on emotional awareness, organizational support, and perceived efficacy[26,88].

Table 4: Field Stories and Supporting Research

Case	Key Strategy	Research Link
Educator	Peer support & mindfulness	Cetin et al.; Doyle et al.
Paramedic	Debriefing & counseling	Greenberg et al.; Fallon et al.
Social Worker	Boundaries & supervision	Savina; Loomis et al.

Conclusion

Resilience does not always look strong. Sometimes it looks like pausing, seeking help, setting limits, and choosing to continue. These stories remind us that survival in high-stress professions is not about enduring alone—it is about building systems of care that allow people to recover and grow.

For individuals and organizations alike, learning from those in the trenches is not optional. Their experiences offer blueprints for transforming trauma exposure into sustained capacity and collective strength.

Chapter 10

Building Individual Resilience

Everyday Practices for Personal Well-Being

Resilience is not just something we bring into our work—it's something we build through what we do outside of it. While systems, teams, and supervisors have a role to play, the foundation of sustainable well-being is deeply personal. It's in the breath we take before speaking. It's in how we sleep, move, reflect, and ask for help.

Helping professionals often fall into the trap of self-sacrifice, believing that endurance alone equals strength. But real resilience is not about pushing through until we break. It's about intentionally caring for the nervous system, tending to relationships, setting boundaries, and reconnecting with our own humanity. This chapter highlights practical, research-supported strategies for restoring energy, preventing burnout, and staying grounded amid the intensity of human-serving work.

Regulating the Nervous System: Breath, Movement, Sleep

The human nervous system is designed to detect and respond to threats—real or perceived. In high-stress professions, this response is often chronically activated, leading to hyperarousal, exhaustion, or emotional dysregulation if not intentionally managed. Everyday practices like intentional breathing, physical activity, and sufficient sleep serve as vital counterbalances, giving the body and mind space to recover and reset[8,98].

In trauma-exposed work, regulation is not simply about stress relief—it is the foundation for trauma recovery. When the nervous system remains in a state of chronic alarm, the brain struggles to integrate difficult experiences into coherent memory. This narrows the "window of tolerance" and increases the likelihood of reactivity, shutdown, or emotional flooding[8].

Regulation practices widen that window, creating space between stimulus and response and restoring a sense of internal safety.

Why Regulation Comes First in Trauma Recovery

Trauma is stored not only in memory but in the body. Without physiological regulation, cognitive strategies such as reframing or reflection have limited impact. Regulation allows professionals to remain present rather than hijacked by survival responses. When the nervous system experiences safety, the brain regains access to reasoning, empathy, and flexibility[98,8].

In helping professions, this capacity is critical. Teachers, clinicians, and first responders must often remain calm in moments of intense emotion. For this reason, regulation is both a personal resilience strategy and a professional competency.

Breathwork: A Reset in Real Time

Breathing is one of the fastest and most accessible ways to regulate the autonomic nervous system. Slow, paced breathing is associated with shifts in autonomic balance and improved emotional regulation, in part through vagal pathways and cardio-respiratory coupling[8,99]. In practical terms, paced breathing can reduce subjective stress and support attention and self-control—especially useful in jobs that require "calm in the moment."

Rather than claiming that a specific branded technique is "proven," research supports the general principle that breathing with longer exhales than inhales supports parasympathetic activation and emotional regulation[99].

Evidence-aligned practice:
Slow-paced breathing (for example, inhaling four seconds and exhaling six to eight seconds) is commonly used to lower arousal

and increase focus. This practice aligns with well-established mechanisms described in the breath-control literature and Polyvagal Theory[8,99].

Breathing practices can be used:

- Before difficult conversations
- After emotionally intense interactions
- During transitions between tasks
- At the end of the workday to signal recovery

Movement: Releasing Tension and Reclaiming Control

Physical activity, even in short bursts, is one of the most reliable methods for decreasing stress and improving emotional regulation. Whether it is walking, yoga, stretching, or dance, movement helps metabolize stress activation and supports mood regulation[100,98].

Teachers, healthcare workers, and first responders often report feeling "frozen" or "trapped" in their bodies during or after escalated encounters. Movement restores agency and embodiment, reminding professionals that they are not defined by the stress they absorb[8].

For educators specifically, wellbeing research increasingly emphasizes feasible "micro-practices"—brief movement, stretching, or transition resets—because time and workload are real constraints[88,89].

Movement also supports trauma recovery by discharging residual activation from the nervous system. Without this discharge, stress accumulates and may emerge later as irritability, fatigue, or emotional numbness.

Sleep: The Most Overlooked Intervention

Chronic sleep deprivation affects cognition, mood, memory, and decision-making. It also heightens the brain's reactivity to threat, impairing emotional regulation and increasing vulnerability to conflict and burnout[98,28]. Helping professionals frequently compromise sleep due to rotating shifts, secondary jobs, or stress-related rumination.

Sleep is not passive rest—it is an active neurological recovery process that consolidates learning, regulates hormones, and restores emotional balance.

Strategies to Improve Sleep:

- Limit screen time at least 30 minutes before bed
- Maintain a consistent sleep schedule, even on weekends
- Create a calming wind-down routine such as journaling, stretching, or breathing
- Reduce caffeine and stimulant use late in the day

Across occupational health research, sleep consistently emerges as a cornerstone of cognitive performance and emotional regulation under chronic stress[98].

Why This Matters in Helping Professions

When individuals neglect basic regulation practices, their "window of tolerance" narrows. Minor frustrations feel overwhelming, and genuine threats may lead to shutdown or explosive responses. On the other hand, tending to the nervous system creates space between stimulus and response—critical in professions where calm presence can prevent harm.

As Polyvagal Theory suggests, safety is not only cognitive—it is biological. When bodies feel safe, people become capable of offering safety to others[8].

Table 1: Quick Tips for Daily Nervous System Care

Practice	Purpose	When to Use
Paced breathing (longer exhale)	Lowers arousal, supports regulation	Before meetings, during stress
Walking or movement breaks	Releases tension, restores attention	Mid-day reset
Stretching	Reconnects body and mind	Between intense tasks
Wind-down routine	Prepares for sleep recovery	Evening

Conclusion

You cannot give what you do not have. Helping professionals are often praised for selflessness, but resilience begins with regulation. Breath, movement, and sleep may seem simple, yet in high-stress professions, they are foundational acts of survival and sustainability.

The Role of Purpose, Boundaries, and Reflection

In high-stress professions, resilience is not merely a personality trait; it is a pattern of behavior rooted in intention. People who sustain themselves in emotionally demanding work do so because they are anchored by purpose, protected by boundaries, and strengthened through reflection[91].

Resilience is not only about recovering from stress—it is about remaining connected to meaning. In trauma-informed systems, purpose acts as an anchor when work feels overwhelming or morally complex.

One of the most overlooked resilience resources is compassion satisfaction—the emotional fulfillment that comes from helping others and feeling competent in one's role[66]. Compassion satisfaction is not incidental; it is protective. Educators and helping professionals who experience higher compassion satisfaction demonstrate lower burnout and stronger engagement, even in high-adversity settings[4,88].

When Purpose Is Shaken: Repairing Meaning After Trauma and Loss

Not all work experiences reinforce purpose. Professionals may encounter situations that violate their values or prevent them from acting as they believe they should. These experiences can fracture meaning and produce moral distress or moral injury[90].

Resilience includes not only finding purpose, but repairing it when it has been shaken.

Meaning repair involves:

- Naming ethical conflict
- Grieving losses or perceived failures
- Reconnecting with core values
- Reframing identity beyond outcomes

Research in healthcare and education shows that professionals who can reinterpret difficult experiences through a values-based lens are more likely to sustain engagement and recover emotionally[101,88].

Boundaries: Sustainable Service

Meaning without boundaries leads to martyrdom. Clear boundaries protect emotional capacity and prevent compassion fatigue and moral injury[64,102].

Boundaries define:

- What is within one's responsibility
- What belongs to the system
- What must be shared or delegated

Healthy boundaries are not detachment; they are sustainability. Professionals who maintain boundaries report lower emotional exhaustion and higher job satisfaction[42,103].

Examples of boundary practices:

- Turning off email after work hours
- Declining tasks outside role scope
- Taking breaks without guilt
- Naming overload early

These actions protect not only individuals but the quality of service they provide.

Reflection: Learning From the Work

Reflection transforms experience into growth. Without it, emotionally demanding work becomes an endless stream of stressors. Reflective practices such as journaling, peer dialogue, and mindfulness help professionals process what they experience and adjust how they carry it[104,42].

Reflective supervision is increasingly used in early childhood and education systems as both a personal resilience tool and an organizational culture shift[39]. Trauma-informed organizational research identifies reflective practice as a buffer against burnout and chronic dysregulation[105].

Daily Practices for Reflective Resilience

- "What aligned with my values today?"
- "What drained me?"
- "What sustained me?"
- "What boundary needs attention?"

Reflection is not rumination; it is structured meaning-making.

The Inner Circle: Social Support and Connection

Social support plays an indispensable role in fostering resilience and mitigating the effects of secondary traumatic stress, burnout, and compassion fatigue[106,91].

For professionals in high-stress roles, connection serves as both emotional protection and professional preservation.

The Protective Role of Social Support

Supportive relationships provide:

- Emotional validation
- Practical assistance
- Psychological safety
- Perspective outside the role

Even the perception of available support improves health outcomes and stress tolerance[106].

Compassion satisfaction is strengthened through relationships that reinforce meaning and reduce isolation[66,4].

Trauma-Specific Peer Support vs General Social Support

Not all support functions equally. Trauma-exposed professionals benefit from structured peer support that includes emotional processing, normalization, and learning.

Table 2: Peer-Support vs. General Social Support

Type of Support	Function	Best For
Family & friends	Emotional refuge	Identity beyond work
Colleagues	Shared understanding	Daily stress
Peer support groups	Trauma processing	Critical incidents
Supervision	Reflection & guidance	Moral distress

Structured peer support programs reduce isolation and improve retention in education and healthcare[88,89,39].

Cultivating Connection Through Organizational Practices

Organizations shape whether a connection becomes culture. Research on psychological safety shows that teams thrive when leaders model empathy and invite feedback without punishment[107].

Trauma-informed organizational frameworks emphasize:

- Shared reflection
- Relational safety
- Team rituals
- Support after crises[26,105]

Expanding Personal Circles of Support

Beyond work, relationships with family and friends provide:

- Emotional grounding
- Identity balance
- Encouragement for self-care

These ties prevent role engulfment and remind professionals they are more than their job.

Conclusion

Social connection is not an accessory to resilience—it is its foundation. Professionals who remain connected to others are more likely to recover, adapt, and endure.

Naming the Work: Journaling, Debriefing, and Reframing

For individuals in high-stress professions, reflective practices such as journaling, debriefing, and cognitive reframing are not optional wellness activities—they are essential tools for processing experiences, preserving emotional capacity, and sustaining professional identity over time[104,42].

Trauma exposure fragments experience. Without intentional reflection, difficult encounters accumulate as unprocessed stress rather than integrated learning. Naming the work—putting language to what has been witnessed and felt—allows professionals to metabolize emotional load rather than carry it silently.

Journaling as a Tool for Emotional Integration

Journaling supports emotional processing and meaning-making by helping individuals organize thoughts, identify patterns, and articulate values. Expressive writing research demonstrates improvements in emotional clarity and health outcomes when individuals reflect on stressful or traumatic experiences[42].

For educators and helping professionals, journaling can:

- Clarify emotional reactions
- Reveal boundary needs
- Track stress accumulation
- Reinforce purpose and learning

Practical prompts include:

- "What am I holding from today?"
- "What challenged me most, and why?"
- "What helped me stay grounded?"
- "What do I want to release before tomorrow?"

Over time, journaling becomes a mirror for self-awareness and a container for experiences that might otherwise overwhelm.

Debriefing for Emotional Release and Learning

Debriefing provides a structured space to process emotionally intense events. When conducted safely and voluntarily, it reduces isolation and supports shared meaning-making[107,26].

Trauma-informed debriefing differs from early crisis intervention models that sought to prevent PTSD. It focuses on:

- Emotional validation
- Reflection
- Learning
- Connection
- Restoration of safety

Research on emergency and trauma-exposed professionals suggests that debriefing is most beneficial when:

- Participation is voluntary
- It is facilitated by trained leaders or peers
- Psychological safety is prioritized

The goal is support rather than forced disclosure[60,105]

Debriefing helps teams transform chaos into coherence and experience into shared understanding.

Reframing to Foster a Constructive Perspective

Reframing is the cognitive process of interpreting events through a more adaptive or values-aligned lens. Rather than denying difficulty, reframing restores agency and reduces helplessness[108,109].

Examples:

Instead of "I failed that family," → "I stayed regulated and compassionate in a hard moment."

Instead of "Today was a disaster," → "We navigated something difficult without losing our values."

Reframing does not mean minimizing pain. It means refusing to define oneself solely by crisis or outcome.

Conclusion

Journaling, debriefing, and reframing are not indulgent extras—they are mechanisms of survival and growth. These practices help professionals convert stress into insight and preserve meaning in emotionally demanding work.

Recognizing When You Need Help (and Asking for It)

In trauma-exposed professions, a dangerous myth persists: strength means self-sufficiency. In reality, resilient professionals are those who recognize when they are nearing limits and seek support early. Barriers to help-seeking are shaped by stigma, fear of judgment, and cultural norms of toughness[110,50,107].

Identifying When Help Is Needed

Early indicators include:

- Emotional numbness or irritability
- Sleep disruption and rumination
- Withdrawal from colleagues or family
- Persistent shame or hopelessness
- Fantasies of escape or quitting

These are not failures. They are nervous system signals that recovery is needed[98,108].

Barriers to Asking for Help

Common barriers include:

- Fear of appearing weak[110]
- Concern about job consequences[107]
- Identity norms in caregiving professions
- Lack of clarity about resources

Stigma thrives in silence. When distress is hidden, it becomes heavier.

What Asking for Help Can Look Like

Help-seeking does not always mean therapy. It may involve:

- Talking with a trusted colleague
- Requesting temporary workload adjustment
- Using peer support or EAP services
- Scheduling counseling before crisis

Simple language can open the door:

- "I'm overwhelmed—can we talk?"
- "I need support right now."
- "I'm not okay, and I don't want to wait until I am."

How Systems Enable or Block Help-Seeking

Psychological safety predicts whether people speak up early[107,111]. Trauma-informed systems make support visible, credible, and accessible[105,73].

Key elements include:

- Leaders modeling vulnerability
- Confidential access to support
- Clear pathways for help
- No penalty for using resources

Key Takeaway

Recovery is not a solo task. Systems that normalize support protect people before collapse occurs.

Self-Care Isn't a Luxury—It's Prevention

Self-care is often trivialized as indulgence. For trauma-exposed professionals, it is personal protective equipment for the nervous system[108,7].

When framed through a trauma-informed lens, self-care becomes both:

an individual practice, and

an organizational obligation[26,105]

Redefining Self-Care

True self-care includes:

- Regulation
- Boundaries
- Recovery
- Reflection
- Joy
- Connection

It is not escape from work but preservation of the capacity to do it well.

Educator wellbeing research shows that self-care must be feasible and supported by leadership, or it becomes another burden[88,89].

Prevention vs Crisis Response

Waiting until distress appears turns self-care into damage control. Prevention involves:

- Daily nervous system care
- Protected rest
- Meaningful connection
- Ongoing reflection[112,51]
- Organizational Responsibility

Organizations shape whether self-care is possible. Trauma-informed systems include:

- Reflective supervision
- Recovery time
- Reasonable workloads
- Leader modeling
- Psychological safety[26,39]
- Core Proactive Practices
- Movement and regulation routines
- Sleep protection
- Boundary enforcement
- Joy and restoration
- Daily self-check-ins

Key Takeaway

Self-care is not indulgence. It is prevention. When framed as infrastructure rather than individual weakness, it sustains both people and mission.

From Recovery to Growth: Sustaining the Self Over Time

Resilience is not a single behavior but a lifelong pattern of recovery and renewal. High-stress work will inevitably include seasons of depletion. What matters is whether individuals and systems know how to move from strain back into stability—and from stability into growth[91].

Trauma recovery is nonlinear. It involves:

- Regulation
- Meaning repair
- Connection
- Support
- Renewal

Over time, these practices build what researchers call post-traumatic growth—the capacity to develop deeper purpose, empathy, and wisdom through adversity[109,110].

Sustaining the self means:

- Accepting vulnerability
- Practicing recovery regularly
- Seeking connection
- Honoring limits
- Preserving identity beyond role

Professionals who remain resilient are not those who avoid pain; they are those who know how to recover.

Table 3: The Resilience Cycle

Phase	Key Practice
Activation	Regulation
Processing	Reflection
Repair	Meaning-making
Support	Connection
Renewal	Rest and purpose

This cycle transforms stress into capacity.

Conclusion

Individual resilience is not heroic endurance. It is practiced recovery. When professionals care for their nervous systems, protect their boundaries, seek support, and rebuild meaning, they create a foundation for long-term service without self-erasure.

Resilience is not about surviving work.
It is about remaining whole within it.

Chapter 11

Building Organizational Resilience

Embedding Well-Being into Systems and Leadership

Resilience is not just an individual skill—it's a collective capacity. While individual strategies help staff manage stress and recover from adversity, real and lasting resilience requires organizations to change the way they function. Trauma-informed care is not a checklist; it is a cultural shift that reimagines how we supervise, support, and sustain people doing hard work in high-pressure environments.

This chapter focuses on how to move from pockets of wellness to embedded resilience strategies that are systemic, equitable, and sustainable. The goal is not simply to prevent burnout, but to design organizations that actively support healing, growth, and long-term engagement. These systems must be grounded in trust, safety, shared purpose, and clear policies that put people first.

Leadership is central to this work. Supervisors and decision-makers set the tone—either reinforcing a culture of silence and overwork or modeling emotional honesty, vulnerability, and shared responsibility. Research shows that staff who perceive their workplaces as supportive and trauma-informed report lower levels of secondary traumatic stress and burnout and higher compassion satisfaction[15,113].

Emerging evidence also supports mindfulness-informed organizational practices when embedded into routines and leadership behaviors rather than framed solely as individual coping strategies[114]. Equity remains central to systemic well-being. Trauma-informed leadership must consider power dynamics, cultural responsiveness, and implicit bias in shaping staff experiences of safety and trust[7].

By embedding reflective supervision, staff-centered policies, and inclusive leadership practices, organizations move beyond individual coping strategies to truly resilient systems.

Trauma-Informed Supervision and Reflective Leadership

In trauma-exposed workplaces, leadership is not only about operational decisions—it is about emotional stewardship. Trauma-informed supervision recognizes that staff carry emotional burdens from both personal and professional experiences. Reflective leadership creates space to process those burdens in supportive, nonjudgmental ways[115,15].

Trauma-informed supervision integrates the principles of safety, trustworthiness, collaboration, empowerment, and cultural humility[7]. Staff who feel emotionally supported by supervisors show lower levels of secondary traumatic stress and greater compassion satisfaction[15].

In practice, this includes:

- Regular check-ins beyond productivity
- Awareness of secondary trauma and emotional strain
- Validation of staff experiences
- Protected time for supervision and reflection
- Clear boundaries with compassion

Reflective leaders slow down conversations and attend to the emotional meaning of work, not only performance metrics. Rather than asking only "What went wrong?", they ask:

- "How did this affect you?"
- "What support do you need?"
- "What did this situation bring up for the team?"

Reflective supervision reduces burnout, strengthens psychological safety, and builds trust[115,39]. Mindfulness-based leadership practices further enhance self-regulation and presence[114].

Training leaders in trauma awareness includes:

- Emotional intelligence[116]
- Recognizing secondary traumatic stress
- Delivering feedback without shame
- Understanding power and privilege in supervision

Modeling healthy boundaries

Without reflective leadership, even well-intentioned supervisors may unintentionally perpetuate stress and disengagement[103].

Key Takeaway
Trauma-informed supervision is not soft leadership—it is protective leadership. When supervision becomes a space of connection rather than correction, organizational resilience increases by design[117,39].

Debriefing, Peer Support, and Staff-Centered Practices

In trauma-exposed systems, staff are often expected to absorb others' pain while suppressing their own. This emotional dissonance increases risk for burnout and moral injury[113]. Debriefing and peer support function as systems of care rather than optional extras[117].

Debriefing provides structured space to process critical incidents through emotional validation and meaning-making[7]. Effective debriefing includes:

- Designated time and space
- Skilled facilitation
- Confidentiality and emotional safety
- Reflection on what happened and what is needed

Debriefing strengthens cohesion and reduces long-term distress[118,39]. Mindfulness-informed approaches further support emotional regulation[114].

Peer support relies on shared experience and trained listeners rather than therapy. Research shows peer support reduces isolation and improves retention in high-stress professions[99,10].

Staff-centered practices embed resilience into daily operations:

- Recovery time after crises
- Flexible scheduling
- Recognition of emotional labor
- Anonymous feedback channels
- Inclusion in decision-making

As Bloom[117] emphasizes, resilience becomes embedded when organizations ask, "What can we change to reduce the need for recovery?"

Key Takeaway
Debriefing and peer support normalize emotional labor and build collective trust.

Normalizing Mental Health Conversations

Silence around mental health is a risk factor. When employees cannot discuss emotional strain, disengagement and burnout rise[119,15]. Psychological safety enables openness without fear of judgment[107,111].

Normalizing mental health conversations includes:

- Leaders modeling vulnerability
- Emotional check-ins during supervision
- Avoiding stigmatizing language
- Offering multiple support pathways
- Protecting staff from professional consequences

Leaders set emotional tone. Over 80% of employees report valuing workplaces that prioritize mental health[10].

Cultural humility is essential. Mental health expression varies across cultures, identities, and histories[7,95]. Trauma-informed organizations:

- Avoid clinical jargon
- Provide multilingual resources
- Acknowledge stigma histories
- Listen without assumptions

Key Takeaway
Normalizing mental health conversations creates safer, more resilient workplaces.

Equity and Inclusion as Resilience Infrastructure

Organizational resilience cannot be separated from equity. Systems that distribute stress unevenly, silence marginalized voices, or ignore historical and structural inequities create conditions in which burnout and moral injury are more likely to occur. In contrast, inclusive organizations that recognize differential burdens and promote fairness build stronger psychological safety and collective endurance.

Resilience is often framed as universal, but the experience of stress is not. Workers who occupy marginalized identities related to race, gender, disability, sexual orientation, or immigration status frequently encounter additional emotional labor through microaggressions, discrimination, and invisibility. These layered stressors compound occupational strain and increase vulnerability to burnout and disengagement[37,41,103].

Trauma-informed organizational frameworks emphasize that safety must be cultural as well as psychological. Inclusion is not simply representation; it is the presence of voice, respect, and meaningful participation in decision-making[7,26]. When staff perceive fairness in workload, discipline, promotion, and recognition, trust increases and emotional exhaustion decreases[107,101].

Equity as resilience infrastructure includes several core practices:

Workload justice: ensuring that emotional labor and crisis response are not disproportionately assigned to the same individuals or groups.

Cultural safety: acknowledging historical trauma and community context in both staff support and service delivery.

Voice and participation: inviting staff into program design, policy review, and recovery planning.

Protection from harm: addressing harassment, bias, and retaliation as threats to psychological safety rather than interpersonal conflicts.

Organizations that fail to address inequity often unintentionally reproduce trauma through their structures. By contrast, those that integrate inclusion into resilience efforts strengthen belonging and moral coherence. Staff who feel seen and protected are more likely to remain engaged during times of stress and disruption.

Equitable resilience-building also requires cultural humility. Leaders must remain open to learning from lived experience rather than assuming that standardized wellness strategies apply equally across diverse communities. Healing practices may be communal, spiritual, or culturally grounded rather than solely clinical. Respecting these differences expands the definition of resilience beyond individual coping and into collective dignity.

In this way, equity is not an accessory to resilience. It is one of its load-bearing walls.

Measuring and Monitoring Organizational Resilience

Resilience is not only a value; it is a condition that can be observed, assessed, and strengthened through feedback. Organizations that sustain wellbeing do not rely on intuition alone. They use data— both quantitative and qualitative—to understand how their workforce experiences stress, support, and safety over time.

Traditional performance metrics such as productivity or compliance offer limited insight into psychological health. Trauma-informed and resilience-oriented organizations expand their evaluation lens to include indicators of emotional climate, trust, and recovery capacity[26,101].

Why Evaluation Matters in Trauma-Exposed Systems

High-pressure environments often normalize dysfunction. Over time, overwork, poor communication, and emotional suppression can become embedded in organizational culture—not because people do not care, but because systems were never designed with staff well-being in mind[117].

Without structured feedback loops, burnout becomes invisible and systemic. Evaluation shifts organizations from reactive crisis management to adaptive learning cultures that evolve based on workforce needs[101,103].

Evaluating through a resilience lens reframes the central question from:

"How are individuals coping?"
to
"How is the system functioning?"

Core Questions for Resilient Organizations

Trauma-informed evaluation asks:

- Do people feel psychologically safe at work?[107]
- Are staff supported after critical incidents or emotional strain?
- Do leaders model healthy boundaries and recovery?
- Are workloads sustainable and fairly distributed?
- Is feedback acknowledged and acted upon?

These questions reflect research on psychological safety, collective efficacy, and organizational well-being[112,73].

Domains Commonly Assessed

Key areas of organizational resilience include:

- Psychological safety and trust
- Burnout and emotional exhaustion
- Turnover and absenteeism
- Access to supervision and peer support
- Help-seeking behaviors
- Perceptions of fairness and inclusion
- Recovery practices after crises

Together, these indicators reveal whether resilience is functioning as infrastructure or remaining symbolic.

Quantitative and Qualitative Tools

Effective evaluation blends standardized measures with narrative feedback. Numbers show patterns; stories reveal meaning.

Table 1: Examples of tools include:

Domain	Indicator	Example Tool
Safety	Trust, openness	Psychological safety scales
Stress	Burnout, fatigue	Burnout inventories
Support	Access to debriefing	Utilization logs
Culture	Belonging	Climate surveys
Equity	Workload fairness	Audits and interviews

Qualitative methods such as focus groups, listening sessions, and exit interviews deepen understanding of how policies are experienced rather than merely whether they exist[39].

These spaces also serve as interventions in themselves by signaling that staff perspectives matter.

Feedback Loops and Learning Systems

Measurement becomes resilience-building only when data leads to action. Feedback loops transform evaluation into learning by asking:

- What patterns are emerging?
- Where are people struggling?
- Which supports are underused or inaccessible?
- What structural changes are needed?

Learning organizations revisit policies and practices based on feedback rather than treating assessment as compliance. This aligns with trauma-informed principles of transparency and continuous improvement[7,26].

When staff see that their input leads to real change—adjusted schedules, new peer supports, revised protocols—trust increases and engagement deepens.

Ethical Use of Resilience Data

Monitoring resilience carries ethical responsibility. Data must never be used to pathologize individuals or justify increased demands. Instead, it should reveal systemic strain and guide protective action.

Key ethical principles include:

- Confidentiality and psychological safety
- Voluntary participation
- Transparency about purpose and findings
- Protection from retaliation or stigma

Resilience metrics should never ask:

"Why can't you handle this?"
but instead:
"What does this tell us about how the system is functioning?"

From Measurement to Meaningful Change

Trauma-informed organizations close the loop with humility and visibility:

- Sharing what was learned (anonymously when needed)
- Naming specific actions and timelines
- Explaining what cannot yet be changed and why
- Continuing dialogue even when feedback is difficult

Visible responsiveness to feedback significantly improves trust, morale, and retention[101,107].

Key Takeaway

Evaluating organizational culture through a resilience lens requires courage, curiosity, and accountability. It transforms resilience from an abstract value into a living practice. By routinely examining how systems affect the people who work within them—and acting on what is learned—organizations create safer, more supportive, and more sustainable environments.

In this way, resilience becomes not merely a goal, but an ongoing process of learning, repair, and growth.

Team Rituals That Reinforce Trust and Purpose

Trust is not built through a single conversation, policy, or training. It emerges through repeated, consistent actions over time. In trauma-informed organizations, small daily and weekly rituals often do more to reinforce psychological safety and shared purpose than formal programs alone. These intentional practices provide rhythm, predictability, and emotional connection—vital anchors in environments where unpredictability and secondary trauma are common[107,39].

When team members know they have reliable spaces to show up authentically and feel seen, they are more likely to stay engaged, support one another, and sustain resilience during challenges[73].

The Power of Ritual in High-Stress Workplaces

A ritual is more than a routine. While routines improve efficiency, rituals create meaning. They deliberately ground people in shared values and belonging, counteracting the disconnection and hypervigilance common in trauma-exposed work[117].

Neuroscience suggests that rituals help regulate stress physiology by reducing ambiguity and activating parasympathetic responses, which calm the body and promote collective emotional attunement[98]. In teams, rituals enhance cohesion, bolster collective efficacy, and improve retention[103].

Examples of effective team rituals include:

- Morning huddles that align goals and create space for emotional check-ins.

- End-of-shift closing circles to debrief and acknowledge both successes and struggles.
- Weekly team meals or informal shared breaks that foster connection.
- Celebrating milestones, such as birthdays, work anniversaries, or project completions.
- Opening meetings with grounding exercises, affirmations, or shared intentions.

When practiced regularly, these become cultural norms—not "extras," but foundational to the emotional health of the team[7].

Recognizing how each person's contribution ties back to the greater purpose.

When purpose is consistently and visibly reaffirmed—not just during onboarding or Key Takeaway

Team rituals are small but powerful levers for fostering connection, reducing burnout, and reinforcing trust, purpose, and shared humanity. When embedded into the regular rhythm of work and designed inclusively, rituals deepen resilience, helping teams thrive even in the face of adversity.

Conclusion: Resilience as Infrastructure, Not Ideology

Organizational resilience is not built through slogans or short-term wellness programs. It is constructed through equitable policies, supportive leadership, relational safety, and learning systems that evolve after a crisis. When institutions measure what matters, honor diversity, and repair harm, resilience becomes embedded rather than aspirational.

The work of rebuilding and strengthening relationships, explored throughout this chapter, is inseparable from the work of justice and accountability. Sustainable resilience requires not only care for individuals but the transformation of the environments in which they serve.

Resilient organizations do not demand endurance.
They design for recovery.
They normalize humanity.
And they grow wiser through adversity.

Chapter 12

Community and Systems

Resilience — From Recovery to Renewal

High-stress professions do not operate in isolation. They exist within communities, institutions, and systems that are repeatedly shaped by crisis, disruption, and change. While individual and organizational resilience are essential, they are insufficient on their own to sustain long-term recovery. True resilience must extend outward—into networks of care, learning systems, and shared responsibility for human well-being.

This chapter focuses on what happens after disruption: how organizations and communities repair trust, restore functioning, and evolve in response to adversity. Resilience at this level is not simply the absence of breakdown; it is the capacity to transform suffering into insight, coordination, and renewed purpose. Drawing on research from healthcare, education, and public service systems, this chapter examines recovery processes, learning cultures, and scalable peer support models as pillars of community and systems resilience[26,101,7].

Recovery After Crisis: Repairing Trust and Function

Crisis alters systems as much as it alters individuals. Whether the disruption involves workplace violence, the death of a student or patient, public controversy, natural disaster, or institutional failure, the aftermath is marked by emotional rupture and organizational instability. Recovery is not automatic. Without intentional processes of repair, organizations risk normalizing dysfunction, silencing distress, and fragmenting trust[117].

Trauma-informed recovery begins with recognition that crises affect collective nervous systems. Fear, shame, and uncertainty spread rapidly through social environments, shaping behavior long after the immediate event has passed[98]. In the absence of clear communication and relational support, staff may disengage, withdraw, or become hypervigilant. These reactions are not signs of weakness but predictable responses to perceived threat and loss of safety[8].

Repairing trust after crisis requires more than returning to routine. It involves restoring three foundational elements: psychological safety, relational connection, and shared meaning[107,101]. Leaders who acknowledge harm openly and invite dialogue signal that the organization can tolerate truth rather than suppress it. This transparency helps interrupt cycles of blame and silence that often follow traumatic events.

Effective recovery processes typically include:

- Structured reflection spaces for staff to process emotional impact and operational lessons.
- Clear communication about what is known, what is uncertain, and what steps are being taken.
- Visible care actions, such as workload adjustments or additional supports after crisis.
- Symbolic repair, including rituals of remembrance, closure, or recommitment to values.

These practices align with trauma-informed principles of safety, trustworthiness, and empowerment[7]. When organizations fail to provide such containment, staff may experience what has been described as secondary institutional trauma—distress not only from the original event but from the system's response to it[26].

Recovery also requires attending to moral injury. Crises often expose ethical fractures, such as situations where professionals feel unable to act in accordance with their values due to systemic constraints[90]. Addressing moral injury involves naming ethical tension, validating emotional conflict, and reaffirming shared purpose. Without this step, resilience efforts risk becoming superficial coping strategies rather than genuine restoration.

In this sense, recovery is not a return to normal. It is a reorientation of relationships, policies, and meaning-making processes so that the system can function with greater wisdom and integrity than before.

Learning Organizations: Turning Breakdown into Growth

Resilient systems are not those that avoid failure; they are those that learn from it. The concept of the learning organization emphasizes adaptive capacity—the ability to reflect on experience, integrate feedback, and evolve practices in response to stress and change[26,101].

In trauma-exposed fields, breakdowns often reveal hidden vulnerabilities: inadequate staffing, unclear protocols, cultural silences, or inequities in workload and voice. When organizations treat crises as aberrations to be forgotten rather than data to be examined, these vulnerabilities persist. Conversely, when disruption becomes a catalyst for inquiry, systems strengthen their capacity for future resilience.

A learning-oriented response reframes crisis from "Who failed?" to "What did this reveal about how we operate?" This shift reduces shame and defensiveness while increasing collective efficacy[107]. It also aligns with trauma-informed values by prioritizing understanding over punishment and growth over blame[7].

Learning organizations engage in several core practices:

- After-action reflection, focusing on both emotional and operational dimensions of events.

- Policy and procedure revision informed by lived experience.
- Training adaptation to address identified gaps in preparedness or communication.
- Staff participation in redesigning systems rather than receiving top-down solutions.

Such practices support what researchers describe as post-traumatic organizational growth—the capacity for institutions to become more humane, transparent, and effective after adversity[101,117].

Importantly, learning must include attention to power and equity. Whose experiences are heard? Whose stress is normalized? Whose labor increases after crisis? Without an equity lens, organizations may unintentionally reinforce the very conditions that contributed to breakdown[103,95].

Learning cultures also protect against repetition of harm. When lessons are integrated into training and leadership development, they become part of organizational memory rather than isolated insights. Over time, this memory forms a resilience archive—a shared understanding of how the system survives and adapts.

In this way, resilience becomes cumulative. Each disruption contributes to a deeper collective capacity for regulation, coordination, and ethical clarity.

Peer Support Models at Scale

One of the most promising developments in systems resilience is the emergence of structured peer support programs. These models recognize that healing and regulation are often most effective when offered by those who share a professional identity and lived experience rather than solely by external clinicians[118,99].

Healthcare systems have pioneered scalable peer support initiatives in response to provider distress following adverse events, workplace violence, and medical error. Programs such as RISE (Resilience in Stressful Events) at Johns Hopkins and Helping Healers Heal at NYC Health + Hospitals train staff to provide emotional first aid, debriefing, and referral to resources[101,117]. These initiatives reduce isolation, normalize emotional response, and strengthen organizational trust.

Peer support works because it operates at the intersection of neuroscience and social identity. Shared experience reduces threat perception and increases relational safety, allowing individuals to remain within their window of tolerance during difficult conversations[8,98]. Rather than pathologizing distress, peer support frames emotional response as a professional reality that deserves acknowledgment and care.

Key elements of effective peer support models include:

- Voluntary participation rather than mandated engagement.
- Clear role boundaries, distinguishing peer support from therapy.
- Training in listening and referral, not problem-solving.
- Leadership endorsement, signaling legitimacy and protection from stigma.
- Ongoing supervision for peer supporters themselves.

While most research on peer support has emerged from healthcare, these frameworks translate readily to other high-stress environments. Schools, emergency services, and public agencies face similar patterns of exposure to trauma, ethical tension, and cumulative stress[88,73]. Adaptation requires attention to context, culture, and available resources rather than replication of medical models.

Scaling peer support also reinforces collective responsibility for well-being. When emotional labor is shared rather than hidden, organizations move away from heroic individualism toward relational resilience. This shift is particularly important in professions that historically reward stoicism and silence.

Peer support is not a substitute for professional mental health care. Instead, it functions as an accessible first layer of response—one that reduces barriers to help-seeking and preserves connection in moments of vulnerability[110,50].

Through these systems of shared care, resilience becomes distributed across networks rather than carried by individuals alone.

Measuring Community and Systems Resilience

Resilience at the community and systems level must be more than an aspiration; it must be observable, assessable, and improvable. Organizations committed to long-term well-being recognize that what is not measured cannot be sustained. However, traditional metrics—such as productivity, attendance, or compliance—capture only surface functioning. Trauma-informed systems expand evaluation to include psychological safety, relational trust, and recovery capacity[26,101].

Measuring resilience requires shifting the central question from "Are people performing?" to "Are people supported?" This reframing acknowledges that human systems function optimally only when emotional health and ethical integrity are protected alongside operational outcomes[7].

Key domains of community and systems resilience include:

- Psychological safety: whether individuals feel safe expressing concern or vulnerability[107].
- Collective efficacy: shared belief in the group's capacity to manage adversity.
- Access to support: availability and utilization of peer and professional resources.
- Equity of burden: whether stress and emotional labor are distributed fairly.
- Recovery processes: presence of structured reflection and repair mechanisms.

Quantitative measures such as climate surveys and burnout inventories reveal trends, but they cannot capture meaning in and of themselves. Qualitative methods such as listening sessions, focus groups, and narrative inquiry provide context and human texture to data[39]. Together, they form a fuller picture of how resilience is lived rather than merely declared.

Ethical measurement is critical. Data must never be used to rank individuals' coping capacity or justify higher demands. Instead, resilience metrics should illuminate systemic strain and guide protective action. Trauma-informed evaluation honors confidentiality, transparency, and voluntary participation, preventing measurement itself from becoming a source of threat or stigma[7].

When organizations share findings openly and describe how changes will follow, measurement becomes an act of care. In this way, evaluation strengthens trust rather than eroding it.

Community Networks, Mutual Aid, and Social Capital

No organization survives crisis alone. Community resilience depends on networks of relationship that extend beyond formal institutions into families, neighborhoods, faith groups, and professional alliances. These connections form what sociologists describe as social capital—the web of trust, reciprocity, and shared responsibility that allows communities to respond to disruption[96].

Mutual aid initiatives exemplify this principle in action. Rather than relying solely on top-down services, mutual aid organizes communities to support one another through shared resources, communication, and care. During disasters, pandemics, and institutional breakdowns, these networks often mobilize more rapidly and sensitively than formal systems[41].

Community networks support resilience in several ways:

- Practical assistance, such as food, transportation, and childcare.
- Emotional containment, reducing isolation during uncertainty.
- Cultural meaning-making, helping groups interpret adversity within shared values.
- Advocacy and voice, ensuring marginalized perspectives are included in recovery efforts.

For trauma-exposed professions, community partnerships provide additional scaffolding. Schools connected to families and service agencies, hospitals linked to neighborhood organizations, and public agencies collaborating with cultural leaders all benefit from expanded capacity for care.

Social capital also protects against despair. When individuals feel embedded in networks larger than themselves, they are more likely to experience belonging and hope, even under strain[97]. These relationships become reservoirs of strength that endure beyond any single crisis.

Importantly, community resilience is not neutral. Power, history, and inequality shape who has access to networks and whose voices are amplified. Trauma-informed community building therefore requires intentional inclusion, cultural humility, and shared leadership rather than assuming unity emerges automatically[7,37].

Innovation, Technology, and the Future of Resilience

As stressors grow more complex—climate change, digital harassment, political polarization, and global health crises—resilience strategies must evolve. Innovation plays a critical role in expanding access to support, training, and connection.

Technology has already reshaped how resilience is built and delivered. Tele-mental health, online peer support groups, mobile wellness applications, and virtual training platforms extend care beyond physical walls. These tools increase reach, especially for rural, under-resourced, or stigmatized populations[101].

However, innovation must remain trauma-informed. Digital tools should enhance connection rather than replace it. They must be designed with attention to privacy, equity, and emotional safety to avoid reinforcing surveillance or burnout cultures.

Emerging innovations in resilience include:

- Virtual peer support communities for high-stress professions.

- Simulation-based training for crisis response and emotional regulation.
- Data-informed wellness systems that guide preventive interventions.
- AI-supported pattern recognition to detect organizational stress trends.
- Hybrid learning models combining in-person and digital resilience training.

The future of resilience will depend not on technology alone, but on how it is integrated into human-centered systems. Innovation should amplify empathy, reflection, and shared responsibility rather than accelerate productivity at the expense of well-being.

Resilient systems remain guided by ethical questions: Who benefits from innovation? Who is excluded? Does this tool reduce suffering or merely mask it? These questions anchor progress in values rather than novelty.

12.7 From Recovery to Renewal: A Collective Vision

At its highest level, community and systems resilience is not merely about surviving disruption. It is about renewal—the capacity to reimagine institutions as places of dignity, safety, and shared purpose.

Renewal requires moving beyond short-term fixes toward long-term transformation. It involves embedding learning, care, and equity into the very architecture of organizations and communities. This transformation is not quick. It unfolds through relationships, reflection, and sustained commitment.

Resilient communities share several defining qualities:

- They normalize vulnerability rather than punish it.
- They treat crisis as information rather than failure.
- They distribute care rather than hoard authority.
- They repair harm rather than deny it.
- They measure success by human flourishing as well as performance.

This vision reframes resilience from an individual trait into a moral and civic responsibility. It recognizes that how we respond to stress reveals who we are as institutions and as societies.

The work of renewal asks a different set of questions:

- How do we want to treat those who serve?
- What kind of culture are we building for the next generation?
- What lessons from suffering will we carry forward?
- How will we protect the human heart of our professions?

When communities and systems commit to these questions, resilience becomes not just a strategy, but a shared identity.

Conclusion

Community and systems resilience represents the final expansion of the resilience arc: from individual regulation, to organizational alignment, to collective renewal. What begins as a skill within a person grows into a culture within institutions and, ultimately, into a shared capacity across communities.

Through recovery processes, learning cultures, peer support, measurement, networks, and innovation, resilience becomes woven into the fabric of social life. It is no longer an emergency response. It becomes a design principle.

These practices prepare the ground for the future—not by eliminating adversity, but by ensuring that adversity does not sever connection, meaning, or hope.

At this level, resilience is no longer about bouncing back. It is about growing forward.

Resilience cannot remain the responsibility of individuals alone. When organizations embed reflection, equity, psychological safety, and structural support into their systems, recovery becomes sustainable rather than reactive. Regulation becomes modeled. Repair becomes normalized. Growth becomes expected.

Yet this work extends beyond formal institutions. Prevention, de-escalation, and resilience shape how people relate to stress, conflict, and one another in every setting—schools and workplaces, homes and neighborhoods, boardrooms and community spaces. These principles influence how leaders respond under pressure, how families repair rupture, and how communities metabolize challenge without fragmenting.

When these skills are learned, practiced, and carried forward, what becomes possible is not simply fewer crises. It is stronger systems and steadier people.

Prevention reshapes environments before harm occurs.
De-escalation restores safety when strain emerges.
Resilience ensures that growth follows adversity rather than collapse.

Together, they form more than a framework. They form a way of living and leading—one that honors vulnerability without surrendering strength, that protects dignity while holding boundaries, and that recognizes regulation as both a personal discipline and a collective responsibility.

The work does not end with this book. It continues wherever someone pauses before reacting. Wherever a leader chooses steadiness over dominance. Wherever a system is redesigned to distribute safety rather than threat. Wherever repair replaces shame.

The future will not be built through endurance alone.

It will be built through growth.
Through connection.
Through shared responsibility for one another's well-being.

And through the steady, practiced choice to regulate, restore, and renew—again and again.

Epilogue:

A Vision for the Future of Prevention, De-escalation, and Resilience

From Reaction to Relationship: What This Book Has Shown Us

Prevention, de-escalation, and resilience are not isolated techniques. They are relational capacities that shape how individuals, organizations, and communities respond to stress, conflict, and human suffering. Throughout this book, a consistent truth has emerged: safety is not created through control alone, but through understanding; stability is not sustained through endurance alone, but through connection; and growth is not achieved through avoidance of adversity, but through skilled engagement with it.

Prevention teaches us to recognize risk before it becomes crisis. De-escalation teaches us how to remain present when emotions rise and systems feel strained. Resilience teaches us how to recover, repair, and continue with integrity. Together, these three domains form a coherent framework for humane and effective practice in high-stress environments.

This work reframes conflict not as failure, but as information. It reframes distress not as weakness, but as a nervous system signal. And it reframes recovery not as an individual responsibility alone, but as a collective obligation.

What emerges is a shift from reaction to relationship: from managing behavior to understanding human experience; from punishment to repair; from burnout to sustainability.

Learning as the Bridge Between Values and Practice

Prevention, de-escalation, and resilience do not develop by instinct alone. They must be learned, practiced, and supported over time. Emotional regulation is a developmental skill. Conflict navigation is a practiced discipline. Recovery from stress is a cultivated capacity. Without structured learning opportunities, people rely on habit and impulse in moments of pressure—precisely when the brain's ability to reason and reflect is most compromised.

Learning provides a shared language for recognizing stress responses, naming emotional needs, and restoring safety. It transforms abstract values into observable behaviors. It allows teams to recognize when regulation is faltering and to intervene early, rather than waiting for a breakdown.

Importantly, these skills are not confined to professional settings. The same principles that help a teacher respond to a dysregulated student also guide a parent navigating a child's emotional distress. The strategies that help healthcare teams recover after critical incidents are the same strategies families use to process grief, conflict, and transition. Prevention, de-escalation, and resilience belong to everyday human life.

When people learn these concepts together, they generate collective competence. They move from isolated coping to shared responsibility. Learning becomes not a one-time event, but a cultural practice, one that affirms that emotional literacy and relational skills are essential to safety and well-being.

The Future of Safe and Humane Systems

The future of effective organizations will not be defined solely by productivity or compliance, but by their capacity to sustain human beings in difficult work. High-stress professions will continue to encounter trauma, conflict, and uncertainty. What will determine success is not the absence of adversity, but the presence of systems capable of responding wisely.

Safe systems are those that anticipate strain rather than deny it. Humane systems recognize emotional labor as real labor. Resilient systems are designed for recovery, not just endurance.

Such systems embed:

- Psychological safety alongside physical safety
- Reflection alongside accountability
- Equity alongside efficiency
- Repair alongside performance

They create structures where asking for help is normalized, where distress is met with understanding rather than stigma, and where leadership models regulation rather than reactivity.

This vision requires a departure from cultures of silence and overwork. It requires replacing the mythology of self-sacrifice with a culture of shared care. In these systems, well-being is not a peripheral program; it is a design principle.

Leadership as Moral and Relational Practice

Leadership in the future of prevention, de-escalation, and resilience will be measured not only by decisions made but by emotional presence demonstrated. Leaders shape the nervous system of organizations. They set the tone for whether fear or trust governs daily interactions.

Trauma-informed leadership does not avoid difficult conversations. It approaches them with curiosity, humility, and regulation. It recognizes that power carries responsibility—not only for outcomes, but for the emotional climate in which those outcomes are pursued.

Such leadership is not performative. It is reflective. It listens. It acknowledges harm. It models repair. And it makes room for growth rather than shame.

In this vision, leadership is not dominance but stewardship. Not control but coherence. Not authority alone, but relational accountability.

Equity, Dignity, and Collective Care

Resilience cannot be separated from justice. Systems that distribute stress unevenly, silence marginalized voices, or ignore historical trauma undermine their own stability. True resilience requires attention to dignity, belonging, and cultural meaning.

The future of prevention, de-escalation, and resilience must be inclusive. It must honor diverse ways of expressing distress and healing. It must recognize that safety is experienced differently across identities and histories. And it must ensure that no group bears a disproportionate share of emotional labor.

Collective care emerges when communities refuse to locate suffering solely within individuals and instead examine the conditions that produce it. In this way, resilience becomes not just survival, but moral coherence.

From Skill to Culture: A Call to Action

The work of prevention, de-escalation, and resilience does not end with individual insight. It continues through organizational policy, leadership practice, and everyday relationships. It requires courage to shift from reactive systems to reflective ones. It requires humility to learn new ways of responding to stress. And it requires commitment to protect those who serve others.

This book offers more than strategies. It offers a way of seeing human behavior through a lens of safety, connection, and capacity. It invites professionals, families, and communities to ask not only, How do we manage crisis? but also, How do we prevent harm? How do we preserve dignity? How do we grow wiser through adversity?

Conclusion: Making Safety Sustainable

High-stress environments do not need more heroics. They need better conditions.

Prevention, de-escalation, and resilience work best when they are treated as a connected system instead of separate initiatives. Prevention reduces unnecessary triggers and lowers baseline stress. De-escalation protects dignity and stops harm when tension rises. Resilience makes recovery real, so the same people are not asked to carry the same weight indefinitely.

The most important shift is moving from a person problem mindset to a conditions mindset. When a situation escalates, it is tempting to locate the cause in someone's attitude, character, or compliance. Sometimes individual choices do matter. But in public-facing work, patterns are rarely random. Stress accumulates. Policies add pressure. Communication breaks down. Leadership signals what is safe to say and what must be hidden. Physical spaces overwhelm already taxed nervous systems. When those conditions remain unchanged, the same conflicts return in different forms.

This book is not asking you to tolerate unsafe behavior. It is asking you to respond in a way that improves outcomes and reduces repeat harm. That includes clear boundaries, predictable procedures, and follow-through. It also includes co-regulation, repair, and a shared commitment to dignity.

If you are a frontline professional, the framework provides you with language and tools to stay grounded and effective under pressure. If you lead teams, it gives you a way to build consistency so people are not forced to invent responses in the moment. If you shape policy, it gives you a lens for asking the right questions: Does this reduce stress or add to it? Does it support regulation or trigger survival? Does it distribute the burden fairly, or quietly place it on the same people again and again?

Sustainable safety is not created by one training or one policy. It is created by a culture that practices awareness, values reflection, and treats recovery as part of the job, not a personal hobby.

Our closing invitation is simple. Use what works here, adapt it to your setting, and keep building. If your organization makes even small changes that lower daily stress and increase clarity and support, the impact will compound. People will feel it. Service quality will improve. And the work will become more survivable for the people doing it.

References

1. Perry, B. D. (2006). Applying principles of neurodevelopment to clinical work. Child and Adolescent Psychiatric Clinics of North America, 15(2), 311–335. https://doi.org/10.1016/j.chc.2005.12.004

2. Felitti, V. J., Anda, R. F., Nordenberg, D., et al. (1998). Relationship of childhood abuse and household dysfunction to leading causes of death in adults. American Journal of Preventive Medicine, 14(4), 245–258. https://doi.org/10.1016/S0749-3797(98)00017-8

3. Leitch, L. (2017). Action steps using ACEs and trauma-informed care: A resilience model. Health & Justice, 5(1), 5. https://doi.org/10.1186/s40352-017-0050-5

4. Ellis, W. R., Dietz, W. H., & Chen, E. (2020). Adverse community experiences and child health. American Journal of Preventive Medicine, 58(1), 132–138. https://doi.org/10.1016/j.amepre.2019.09.004

5. Herman, K. C., Hickmon-Rosa, J. E., & Reinke, W. M. (2018). Empirically derived profiles of teacher stress, burnout, self-efficacy, and coping and associated student outcomes. Journal of positive behavior interventions, 20(2), 90-100.

6. Ellis, W. R. (2020). A public health approach to preventing adverse childhood experiences. Journal of Prevention & Intervention in the Community, 48(2), 93–104. https://doi.org/10.1080/10852352.2019.1674994

7. SAMHSA. (2014). Trauma-informed care in behavioral health services (Treatment Improvement Protocol Series 57). U.S. Department of Health and Human Services.

8. Porges, S. W. (2011). The polyvagal theory. W. W. Norton & Company.

9. Perry, B. D., Pollard, R. A., Blakley, T. L., Baker, W. L., & Vigilante, D. (1995). Childhood trauma and the neurobiology of adaptation. Infant Mental Health Journal, 16(4), 271–291. https://doi.org/10.1002/1097-0355(199524)16:4<271::AID-IMHJ2280160404>3.0.CO;2-B

10. American Psychological Association. (2022). Anxiety. https://www.apa.org/topics/anxiety

11. Arnsten, A. F. T. (2009). Stress signalling pathways that impair prefrontal cortex structure and function. Nature Reviews Neuroscience, 10(6), 410–422. https://doi.org/10.1038/nrn2648

12. Teicher, M. H., Samson, J. A., Anderson, C. M., & Ohashi, K. (2022). The effects of childhood maltreatment on brain structure. American Journal of Psychiatry, 179(1), 24–34. https://doi.org/10.1176/appi.ajp.2021.21010068

13. McEwen, B. S. (2017). Neurobiological and systemic effects of chronic stress. Annual Review of Medicine, 68, 49–63. https://doi.org/10.1146/annurev-med-052915-021956

14. Davidson, R. J., & McEwen, B. S. (2012). Social influences on neuroplasticity. Nature Neuroscience, 15(5), 689–695. https://doi.org/10.1038/nn.3093

15. Li, K., Perrault, A., DeYoung, W. A., Cameron, E., Miller, C. T., O'Connor, A. S., ... & Braun, B. (2025). Impact of biophilic

design on college student perception of mental health and environmental benefits: A dose-response study. *Building and Environment*, *267*, 112318. https://doi.org/10.1016/j.buildenv.2024.112318

16. Delgado, R., Stefancic, J., & Liendo, E. (2019). Critical race theory: An introduction (3rd ed.). NYU Press.

17. Bronfenbrenner, U. (1977). Toward an experimental ecology of human development. American Psychologist, 32(7), 513–531. https://doi.org/10.1037/0003-066X.32.7.513

18. Mallett-Smith, S., Jadalla, A., Hardan-Khalil, K., Sarff, L., & Brady, M. (2023). Implementation of an assault prevention quality improvement initiative in an urban emergency department. Journal of Nursing Care Quality, 38(4), 341–347. https://doi.org/10.1097/NCQ.0000000000000711

19. Southwick, S. M., Bonanno, G. A., Masten, A. S., Panter-Brick, C., & Yehuda, R. (2014). Resilience definitions, theory, and challenges: interdisciplinary perspectives. European journal of psychotraumatology, 5(1), 25338. https://doi.org/10.3402/ejpt.v5.25338

20. Hughes, K., Bellis, M. A., Hardcastle, K. A., et al. (2021). The effect of multiple adverse childhood experiences on health. The Lancet Public Health, 6(3), e209–e216. https://doi.org/10.1016/S2468-2667(20)30252-1

21. Shonkoff, J. P., Garner, A. S., Siegel, B. S., et al. (2012). The lifelong effects of early childhood adversity and toxic stress. Pediatrics, 129(1), e232–e246. https://doi.org/10.1542/peds.2011-2663

22. Sue, D. W., Capodilupo, C. M., Torino, G. C., Bucceri, J. M., Holder, A. M., Nadal, K. L., & Esquilin, M. (2007). Racial microaggressions in everyday life. American Psychologist, 62(4), 271–286. https://doi.org/10.1037/0003-066X.62.4.271

23. Armistead, S. L. (2023). Trauma-informed practices in the elementary classroom: Training modules for pre-service teachers (Honors thesis, University of Mississippi). https://egrove.olemiss.edu/hon_thesis/3014

24. Siegel, D. J. (2012). The developing mind (2nd ed.). Guilford Press.

25. National Academy of Medicine. (2019). Taking action against clinician burnout. National Academies Press.

26. Bloom, S. L., & Farragher, B. (2013). Restoring sanctuary: A new operating system for trauma-informed systems of care. Oxford University Press.

27. van der Kolk, B. (2014). The body keeps the score. Viking.

28. Ellis, W. R., & Dietz, W. H. (2017). A new framework for addressing adverse childhood and community experiences. Academic Pediatrics, 17(7), S86–S93. https://doi.org/10.1016/j.acap.2016.07.013

29. Desautels, L. (2019). The role of emotion co-regulation in discipline. Edutopia. https://www.edutopia.org

30. Burgoon, J. K., Buller, D. B., & Woodall, W. G. (1996). Nonverbal communication: The unspoken dialogue (2nd ed.). McGraw-Hill.

31. Kleinsmith, A., & Bianchi-Berthouze, N. (2013). Affective body expression perception. IEEE Transactions on Affective Computing, 4(4), 419–431. https://doi.org/10.1109/T-AFFC.2013.28

32. Davidson, R. J. (2003). Affective neuroscience and psychophysiology: Toward a synthesis. Psychophysiology, 40(5), 655-665.

33. Hölzel, B. K., Carmody, J., Vangel, M., et al. (2011). Mindfulness practice leads to increases in regional brain gray matter density. Psychiatry Research: Neuroimaging, 191(1), 36–43. https://doi.org/10.1016/j.pscychresns.2010.08.006

34. Eisenberger, N. I., Lieberman, M. D., & Williams, K. D. (2003). Does rejection hurt? Science, 302(5643), 290–292. https://doi.org/10.1126/science.1089134

35. Shanafelt, T. D., West, C. P., Sinsky, C., et al. (2023). Changes in burnout and satisfaction among healthcare workers. Mayo Clinic Proceedings, 98(1), 45–58. https://doi.org/10.1016/j.mayocp.2022.09.020

36. Edmondson, A. (1999). Psychological safety and learning behavior in work teams. Administrative Science Quarterly, 44(2), 350–383. https://doi.org/10.2307/2666999

37. Bloom, S. L. (2006). Creating sanctuary: Toward the evolution of sane societies. Routledge.

38. Huo, Y., Couzner, L., Windsor, T., Laver, K., Dissanayaka, N., Cations, M., … & Implementation Science Communications Investigators. (2023). Barriers and enablers for the implementation of trauma-informed care in healthcare settings: A

systematic review. Implementation Science Communications, 4, Article 49. https://doi.org/10.1186/s43058-023-00428-0

39. Loomis, A. M., Coffey, R., Mitchell, J., & Musson Rose, D. (2024). Reflective supervision as trauma-informed organizational change. Reflective Practice, 25(3), 267–285. https://doi.org/10.1080/14623943.2024.2309884

40. Christensen, S. S., Lassche, M., Banks, D., Smith, G., & Inzunza, T. M. (2022). Reducing patient aggression through a nonviolent patient de-escalation program: A descriptive quality improvement process. Worldviews on Evidence-Based Nursing, 19(4), 297-305. https://doi.org/10.1111/wvn.12540

41. Shonkoff, J. P., Slopen, N., & Williams, D. R. (2021). Early childhood adversity, toxic stress, and the impacts of racism on the foundations of health. Annual review of public health, 42(1), 115-134. https://doi.org/10.1146/annurev-publhealth-090419-101940

42. Maslach, C., & Leiter, M. P. (2016). Burnout: A multidimensional perspective. Psychology Press.

43. Olmedo, A., & Muir, J. (2025). Beyond crisis: Enhancing behavioral response through a conceptual framework. Journal of the American Psychiatric Nurses Association, 31(2), 111–120; https://doi.org/10.1177/10783903251315947

44. Rajwani, A., Clark, N., & Montalvo, C. (2023). Understanding best practices in implementation of behavioral emergency response teams through a scoping review. Journal of the American Psychiatric Nurses Association, 29(5), 375-388. https://doi.org/10.1177/10783903221114335

45. Wong, A. H., Ray, J. M., Cramer, L. D., Brashear, T. K., Eixenberger, C., McVaney, C., ... & Venkatesh, A. K. (2022). Design and implementation of an agitation code response team in the emergency department. Annals of emergency medicine, 79(5), 453-464.

46. Hamm, B., Pozuelo, L., & Brendel, R. (2022). General hospital agitation management: leadership theory and health care team best practices using TeamSTEPPS. Journal of the Academy of Consultation-Liaison Psychiatry, 63(3), 213–224.

47. Madigan, D. J., Kim, L. E., Glandorf, H. L., & Kavanagh, O. (2023). Teacher burnout and physical health: A systematic review. International Journal of Educational Research, 119, 102173.https://doi.org/10.1016/j.ijer.2023.102173

48. Eber, L., Barrett, S., Perales, K., Pearsall-Jeffrey, J., Pohlman, K., Putnam, R., ... & Weist, M. D. (2020). Advancing Education Effectiveness: Interconnecting School Mental Health and School-Wide PBIS.

49. Whitecross, F., Lee, S., Bushell, H., Kang, M., Berry, C., Hollander, Y., Sonmez, G., & Rauchberger, I. (2020). Implementing a psychiatric behaviours of concern team can reduce restrictive intervention use and improve safety in inpatient psychiatry. Australasian Psychiatry, 28(4), 401–406. https://doi.org/10.1177/1039856220917072

50. Clement, S., Schauman, O., Graham, T., Maggioni, F., Evans-Lacko, S., Bezborodovs, N., ... & Thornicroft, G. (2015). What is the impact of mental health-related stigma on help-seeking? A systematic review of quantitative and qualitative studies. Psychological medicine, 45(1), 11-27. https://doi.org/10.1017/S0033291714000129

51. West, C. P., Dyrbye, L. N., Erwin, P. J., & Shanafelt, T. D. (2016). Interventions to prevent and reduce physician burnout: A systematic review and meta-analysis. The Lancet, 388(10057), 2272–2281. https://doi.org/10.1016/S0140-6736(16)31279-X

52. Agyapong, V. I. O., Obuobi-Donkor, G., Burback, L., & Wei, Y. (2022). Stress, burnout, anxiety and depression among teachers: A scoping review. Frontiers in Psychology, 13, 836828. https://doi.org/10.3389/fpsyg.2022.836828

53. Bennett, J. M., & Bennett, M. J. (2021). Developing intercultural competence: A guidebook for educators (3rd ed.). Routledge.

54. Morrison, E. W., & Milliken, F. J. (2000). Organizational silence: A barrier to change and development in a pluralistic world. *Academy of Management review*, *25*(4), 706-725.

55. Treviño, L. K., den Nieuwenboer, N. A., & Kish-Gephart, J. J. (2014). (Un)ethical behavior in organizations. Annual Review of Psychology, 65, 635–660. https://doi.org/10.1146/annurev-psych-113011-143745

56. Olmedo, A., & Muir, J. (2026). De-escalation grounded in nursing science: A proposed change to de-escalation curriculum. Advancing Medical-Surgical Nursing, 2, 100038. https://doi.org/10.1016/j.amsn.2025.100038

57. Jones, N., Decker, V. B., & Houston, A. (2023). De-escalation training for managing patient aggression in high-incidence care areas. Journal of Psychosocial Nursing and Mental Health Services, 61(8), 17–24.

58. Somani, R., Muntaner, C., Hillan, E., Velonis, A. J., & Smith, P. (2021). A systematic review: effectiveness of interventions to

de-escalate workplace violence against nurses in healthcare settings. Safety and Health at Work, 12(3), 289–295.

59. Eltrass, G. A. A., Abdelfattah, S. R., Mourad, G. M., Shaban, M., & El-Fatah, W. O. A. (2026). The effect of de-escalation simulation training on empowerment and confidence in managing patient aggression among psychiatric nursing students: an experiential learning approach. BMC nursing, 25(1), 26. https://doi.org/10.1186/s12912-03958-1.

60. Jennings, P. A., & Greenberg, M. T. (2009). The prosocial classroom: Teacher social and emotional competence in relation to student outcomes. Review of Educational Research, 79(1), 491–525. https://doi.org/10.3102/0034654308325693

61. Goleman, D. (1995). Emotional intelligence. Bantam Books.

62. McEwen, B. S., & Akil, H. (2020). Revisiting the stress concept. Neuropsychopharmacology, 45(1), 26–42. https://doi.org/10.1038/s41386-019-0528-6

63. Shields, G. S., Sazma, M. A., & Yonelinas, A. P. (2016). The effects of acute stress on core executive functions. Trends in Cognitive Sciences, 20(7), 459–466. https://doi.org/10.1016/j.tics.2016.04.006

64. Fein, R. A., Vossekuil, B., Pollack, W. S., Borum, R., Modzeleski, W., & Reddy, M. (2002). Threat assessment in schools: A guide to managing threatening situations and to creating safe school climates. U.S. Secret Service & U.S. Department of Education.

65. Shapiro, J., & Galowitz, P. (2016). Peer support for clinicians. Academic Medicine, 91(9), 1200–1204. https://doi.org/10.1097/ACM.0000000000001297

66. Stamm, B. H. (2010). The concise ProQOL manual. Pocatello, ID: ProQOL.org.

67. Hydon, S., Wong, M., Langley, A. K., Stein, B. D., & Kataoka, S. H. (2015). Preventing secondary traumatic stress in educators. Child and Adolescent Psychiatric Clinics of North America, 24(2), 319–333. https://doi.org/10.1016/j.chc.2014.11.003

68. Walker, V. L., Conradi, L. A., Strickland-Cohen, M. K., & Johnson, H. N. (2023). School-wide positive behavioral interventions and supports and students with extensive support needs: A scoping review. International Journal of Developmental Disabilities, 69(1), 13-28. https://doi.org/10.1080/20473869.2022.2116232

69. Cornell, D. G., & Sheras, P. L. (2006). Guidelines for responding to student threats of violence. Sopris West.

70. Watson, A. C., & Compton, M. T. (2019). What research on crisis intervention teams tells us. Journal of the American Academy of Psychiatry and the Law, 47(4), 422–426. https://doi.org/10.29158/JAAPL.003885-19

71. Kolb, D. A. (1984). Experiential learning: Experience as the source of learning and development. Prentice Hall.

72. Çetin, G., Frank, J. L., & Jennings, P. A. (2025). Teacher Self-Efficacy Beliefs and Burnout: The Mediating Roles of Interpersonal Mindfulness in Teaching and Emotion Regulation. Journal of Emotional and Behavioral Disorders, 33(2), 81-98.

73. Pérez, J. E. (2024). Leading with vulnerability: Exploring the effects on perceptions of psychological safety and leader competence (Doctoral dissertation, The George Washington University). ProQuest Dissertations & Theses Global.

https://www.proquest.com/openview/80cceee5aeb79816eeffb4f
f1fea32d6

74. Roberts, A. R., & Ottens, A. J. (2005). The seven-stage crisis intervention model. Brief Treatment and Crisis Intervention, 5(4), 329–339. https://doi.org/10.1093/brief-treatment/mhi030

75. Ting-Toomey, S., & Oetzel, J. G. (2001). *Managing intercultural conflict effectively* (Vol. 5). Sage.

76. Anda, R. F., Felitti, V. J., Bremner, J. D., Walker, J. D., Whitfield, C., Perry, B. D., Dube, S. R., & Giles, W. H. (2006). The enduring effects of abuse and related adverse experiences in childhood. European Archives of Psychiatry and Clinical Neuroscience, 256(3), 174–186. https://doi.org/10.1007/s00406-005-0624-4

77. Stanley, B., & Brown, G. K. (2012). Safety planning intervention: A brief intervention to mitigate suicide risk. Cognitive and Behavioral Practice, 19(2), 256–264. https://doi.org/10.1016/j.cbpra.2011.01.001

78. Borum, R., Fein, R., Vossekuil, B., & Berglund, J. (1999). Threat assessment: defining an approach for evaluating risk of targeted violence. Behavioral sciences & the law, 17(3), 323–337. https://doi.org/10.1002/(sici)1099-0798(199907/09)17:3<323::aid-bsl349>3.0.co;2-g.

79. Sacco, T. L., Ciurzynski, S. M., & Harvey, M. E. (2015). Inpatient workplace violence: Resources for prevention and intervention. Nursing Management, 46(9), 44–51. https://doi.org/10.1097/01.NUMA.0000471914.08554.2c
Shaikh, O., Chai, V. E., Gelfand, M., Yang, D., & Bernstein, M. S. (2024, May). Rehearsal: Simulating conflict to teach conflict

resolution. In Proceedings of the 2024 CHI Conference on Human Factors in Computing Systems (pp. 1-20).

80. Ko, S. J., Ford, J. D., Kassam-Adams, N., Berkowitz, S. J., Wilson, C., Wong, M., & Layne, C. M. (2008). Creating trauma-informed systems. Professional Psychology: Research and Practice, 39(4), 396–404. https://doi.org/10.1037/0735-7028.39.4.396

81. Bryson, S. A., Gauvin, E., Jamieson, A., Rathgeber, M., Faulkner-Gibson, L., Bell, S., & Burke, S. (2020). What are effective strategies for implementing trauma-informed care in youth inpatient psychiatric and residential treatment settings? A realist systematic review. International Journal of Mental Health Systems, 14(1), Article 36. https://doi.org/10.1186/s13033-020-00375-7

82. Determan, J., Horne, M., & Campbell, M. (2019). Trauma-informed design in healthcare environments. Health Environments Research & Design Journal, 12(3), 45–59. https://doi.org/10.1177/1937586719832914

83. Figley, C. R. (1995). Compassion fatigue. Brunner/Mazel.

84. Miller, J. B., & Stiver, I. P. (1997). The healing connection: How women form relationships in therapy and in life. Beacon Press.

85. West, M. A., Eckert, R., Collins, B., & Chowla, R. (2017). Caring to change: How compassionate leadership can stimulate innovation in health care. The King's Fund.

86. Machtinger, E. L., Cuca, Y. P., Khanna, N., et al. (2015). Trauma-informed care in health settings. Women's Health Issues, 25(3), 193–197. https://doi.org/10.1016/j.whi.2015.01.002

87. Green, B. L., Albanese, B. J., Shapiro, N. M., & Aarons, G. A. (2014). The roles of individual and organizational factors in burnout among community-based mental health service providers. Psychological Services, 11(1), 41–49. https://doi.org/10.1037/a0035299

88. Berger, C., Quiroz, R., Ali, N., & Goodwin, L. (2022). In the trauma-informed care trenches: Teacher compassion satisfaction, secondary traumatic stress, burnout, and intent to leave. School Mental Health, 14, 478–491. https://doi.org/10.1007/s12310-021-09469-9

89. Hascher, T., & Waber, J. (2021). Teacher well-being: A systematic review. Educational Research Review, 34, 100411. https://doi.org/10.1016/j.edurev.2021.100411

90. Litz, B. T., Stein, N., Delaney, E., et al. (2009). Moral injury and moral repair in war veterans. Clinical Psychology Review, 29(8), 695–706. https://doi.org/10.1016/j.cpr.2009.08.003

91. Southwick, S. M., & Charney, D. S. (2018). Resilience: The science of mastering life's greatest challenges (2nd ed.). Cambridge University Press.

92. Mealer, M., Jones, J., Newman, J., McFann, K. K., Rothbaum, B., & Moss, M. (2012). The presence of resilience is associated with a healthier psychological profile in intensive care unit (ICU) nurses: results of a national survey. International journal of nursing studies, 49(3), 292-299.

93. Henshall, C., Davey, Z., & Jackson, D. (2020). Nursing resilience interventions—A way forward in challenging healthcare territories. Journal of clinical nursing, 29(19-20), 3597-3609.

94. Greenberg, N., Weston, D., Hall, C., Caulfield, T., Williamson, V., & Fong, K. (2021). Mental health of staff working in intensive care during Covid-19. Occupational medicine, 71(2), 62-67. https://doi.org:10.1093/occmed/kqaa220

95. Patrick, P., Reupert, A., Berger, E., Morris, Z., Diamond, Z., Hammer, M., ... & Fathers, C. (2024). Initiatives for promoting educator wellbeing: a Delphi study. BMC psychology, 12, 220. https://doi.org/10.1186/s40359-024-01724-7

96. Ungar, M. (2008). Resilience across cultures. British Journal of Social Work, 38(2), 218–235.

97. Wexler, L. (2009). The importance of identity, history, and culture in youth resilience. American Journal of Community Psychology, 44, 343–352.

98. McEwen, B. S. (2007). Physiology and neurobiology of stress and adaptation. Physiological Reviews, 87(3), 873–904. https://doi.org/10.1152/physrev.00041.2006

99. Zaccaro, A., Piarulli, A., Laurino, M., et al. (2018). How breath-control can change your life. Frontiers in Human Neuroscience, 12, 353. https://doi.org/10.3389/fnhum.2018.00353

100. Salmon, P. (2001). Effects of physical exercise on anxiety, depression, and sensitivity to stress: a unifying theory. *Clinical psychology review, 21*(1), 33-61.

101. Shanafelt, T., Trockel, M., Rodriguez, A., & Logan, D. (2021). Wellness-centered leadership. Academic Medicine, 96(5), 641–651. https://doi.org/10.1097/ACM.0000000000003907

102. Siegel, D. J. (2010). The mindful brain. Norton.

103. Ueda, N., Kezar, A., Holcombe, E., Vigil, D., & Harper, J. (2024). Emotional labor: Institutional responsibility and strategies to offer emotional support for leaders engaging in diversity, equity, and inclusion work. AERA Open, 10, https://doi.org/10.1177/23328584241296092

104. LeDoux, J. (2015). Anxious: Using the brain to understand and treat fear and anxiety. Viking.

105. Bloom, S. L. (2010). Organizational stress as a barrier to trauma-informed service delivery. Traumatology, 16(4), 44–54.

106. Cohen, S., & Wills, T. A. (1985). Stress, social support, and the buffering hypothesis. Psychological Bulletin, 98(2), 310–357. https://doi.org/10.1037/0033-2909.98.2.310

107. Edmondson, A. C., & Lei, Z. (2014). Psychological safety: The history, renaissance, and future. Annual Review of Organizational Psychology and Organizational Behavior, 1, 23–43. https://doi.org/10.1146/annurev-orgpsy-031413-091305

108. Durlak, J. A., Mahoney, J. L., & Boyle, A. E. (2011). Social and emotional learning: A meta-analysis of school-based interventions. Child Development, 82(1), 405–432. https://doi.org/10.1111/j.1467-8624.2010.01564.x

109. Doidge, N. (2007). The brain that changes itself. Viking.

110. Corrigan, P. (2004). How stigma interferes with mental health care. American Psychologist, 59(7), 614–625. https://doi.org/10.1037/0003-066X.59.7.614

111. Frazier, M. L., Fainshmidt, S., Klinger, R. L., et al. (2017). Psychological safety: A meta-analytic review. Personnel Psychology, 70(1), 113–165. https://doi.org/10.1111/peps.12183

112. Grawitch, M. J., Ballard, D. W., & Erb, K. R. (2015). Psychologically healthy workplaces and stress management. Stress and Health, 31(4), 264–273. https://doi.org/10.1002/smi.2626

113. O'toole, C., & Dobutowisch, M. (2023). The courage to care: Teacher compassion predicts more positive attitudes toward trauma-informed practice. Journal of Child & Adolescent Trauma, 16(1), 123-133. https://doi.org/10.1007/s40653-022-00486-x

114. Sharp, J. E., & Jennings, P. A. (2016). Strengthening teacher presence through mindfulness. Mindfulness, 7(1), 79–89. https://doi.org/10.1007/s12671-015-0421-0

115. Knight, C. (2021). Trauma-informed supervision. In K. O'Donoghue & L. Engelbrecht (Eds.), The Routledge handbook of social work supervision (pp. 410–425). Routledge.

116. Mayer, J. D., Salovey, P., Caruso, D. R., & Sitarenios, G. (2001). Emotional intelligence as a standard intelligence. *Emotion, 1(3), 232–242*. https://doi.org//1528-3542.1.3.232

117. Bloom, S. L. (2023). A biocratic paradigm: Exploring the complexity of trauma-informed leadership and creating presence. Behavioral Sciences, 13(5), 355. https://doi.org/10.3390/bs13050355

118. Mitchell, J. T., & Everly Jr, G. S. (2000). Critical Incident Stress Management and Critical Incident Stress Debriefings: evolutions, effects and. *Psychological debriefing: Theory, practice and evidence*, 71.

119. Blodgett, C., & Lanigan, J. (2018). The association between adverse childhood experiences and school outcomes. School Psychology Quarterly, 33(1), 137–146. https://doi.org/10.1037/spq0000256

About the Authors

About Sheila Mallett-Smith, DNP, RN, LNCC

Dr. Sheila Mallett-Smith is a clinician, educator, and author whose professional life has centered on creating safer, more humane environments in high-stress systems. With more than 35 years of experience in emergency and behavioral health care, she has worked at the intersection of crisis response, trauma-informed practice, and organizational safety.

She previously served as Clinical Nursing Director of Emergency Services at Los Angeles General Medical Center, where she oversaw Trauma, Adult, Pediatric, and Psychiatric Emergency Departments; the Emergency Department Behavioral Response Team; Observation Units; Urgent Care; and associated specialty clinics. In these roles, she led multidisciplinary teams through some of the most complex and emotionally charged clinical environments in the country.

Dr. Mallett-Smith earned her Bachelor of Science in Nursing from BIOLA University, her Master of Science in Nursing Administration from UCLA, and her Doctor of Nursing Practice from California State University, Long Beach. Her award-winning doctoral project achieved a greater than 50 percent reduction in patient-to-staff physical assaults by implementing evidence-based prevention and de-escalation strategies.

She is the creator of the Assault Reduction and Risk for Violence Screening Tool, designed to identify early warning signs and reduce escalation risk in healthcare settings. She has authored and co-authored multiple publications on workplace violence prevention, emergency care, and behavioral health, and currently serves as principal or co-investigator on research initiatives related to safety and emergency department operations.

In 2024, she was appointed to the Riverside County Behavioral Health Commission, where she works to align frontline realities with systemwide strategies that strengthen community safety and care.

Through her work in *PDR: Strategies for Navigating Adversity*, Dr. Mallett-Smith brings a clinical, human-centered lens to Prevention, De-escalation, and Resilience (PDR), translating neuroscience and frontline experience into practical frameworks for healthcare, education, and organizational leadership.

About Jiles Smith II

Jiles Smith II is a social scientist, author, and organizational leader whose life's work centers on resilience, ethical leadership, and systemic prevention. With more than three decades of experience in claims, risk management, compliance, and enterprise safety, he has developed a rare perspective on how individuals and institutions respond to adversity under pressure.

Beginning his career as a claims adjuster and advancing to Director of Risk Management, Smith witnessed firsthand how conflict, crisis, and regulatory complexity shape organizational culture. As Chief Executive Officer of JS Risk Consulting, he partners with public agencies, educational institutions, and community organizations to design prevention-oriented systems that reduce harm, strengthen compliance, and build long-term resilience.

Smith holds an MBA with a specialization in Risk Management from Concordia University. Twice appointed by California governors to serve on the State Fraud Assessment Commission, he has overseen statewide funding initiatives to combat insurance fraud. As Chair of the Equal Opportunity Commission for San Bernardino County, he advanced policies focused on equity, dignity, and social justice.

He is the author of *Risk Management Reimagined*, a forward-looking exploration of modern enterprise risk strategy grounded in ethics and systems thinking, and *Running the Curve*, a leadership guide that blends athletic discipline, strategic foresight, and resilience principles to help individuals and organizations anticipate and adapt to change. His earlier work, *Lessons from Nietzsche for the Modern Soul*, reflects his enduring belief that adversity can catalyze growth, authenticity, and meaningful transformation.

Raised in Compton, California, Smith's commitment to prevention and resilience is both professional and personal. He has founded community-based initiatives serving more than 500 families through nutrition programs, educational workshops, youth town halls, and record expungement fairs that expand opportunity and access. He also hosts a television program addressing mental health, education, and social equity.

Through his writing, public service, and consulting work, Smith advocates for systems that honor human dignity while building strength at every level — individual, organizational, and community.

About the Smith & Smith Collaborative

Together, Dr. Mallett-Smith and Smith developed the Prevention, De-escalation, and Resilience (PDR) framework as an integrated, operational approach to safety and growth in high-stress systems. Drawing from clinical practice, risk management, neuroscience, public policy, and lived experience, their collaborative work bridges frontline realities with systemic design. Their books and training programs are grounded in a shared conviction: that safety is not accidental, resilience is not innate, and dignity is not optional. Through their writing and teaching, they seek to equip leaders, professionals, and communities with practical tools to regulate before reacting, prevent harm before crisis, and grow forward together.